OUR HIDE AND SEEK GOD
Priesthood and the Word of God

Our Hide and Seek God
Priesthood and the Word of God

Michael Neary

With a Foreword by
MOST REV. JOSEPH CASSIDY, D.D.
ARCHBISHOP OF TUAM

A Liturgical Press Book

 THE LITURGICAL PRESS
Collegeville, Minnesota

Dedication

With gratitude and love, I dedicate this book
to my Parents and Family
from whom I have learnt and continue to learn the
unfathomable riches of Priesthood and God's word.
Tom and Nora
Mary, Helen and Noreen

Cover design by Mary Jo Pauly

Scripture quotations are taken from the Revised Standard Version Bible, Catholic Edition, © 1965 and 1966 by the Division of Christian Education of the National Council of Churches of Christ in the USA and used by permission.

Psalms are taken from the *Grail Breviary Psalter,* © The Grail (England) 1966, first published by Geoffrey Chapman. Used by permission of A. P. Watt Limited on behalf of The Grail, England.

1   2   3   4   5   6   7   8   9

Library of Congress Cataloging-in-Publication Data
Neary, Michael.
    Our hide and seek God : priesthood and the word of God / Michael Neary ; with a foreword by Joseph Cassidy, D.D. Archbishop of Tuam.
        p.   cm.
    Includes bibliographical references.
    ISBN 0-8146-2085-X
    1. Pastoral theology—Catholic Church.   2. Catholic Church-
-Clergy.   I. Title.
BX1913.N43   1992
248.8'92—dc20   92-8768
                                                                          CIP

Contents

Foreword

I think it's true to say that most priests don't read much nowadays. It might be more accurate to say that most priests don't have the time or inclination for serious reading anyway. A little reading before we sleep, a little more before we preach, that by and large seems to be the priestly pattern. In addition to that a considerable number of priests express increasing dissatisfaction with the preached diocesan retreat. The social or fraternal value would still be there but the spiritual yield would be disappointingly meagre. It's not unusual to hear a priest saying 'to tell the truth, I don't get much out of it'.

Fr Michael Neary's book is a God-send to the priest who reads only occasionally and to the man who wants more from the preached retreat. It's a God-send to the occasional reader in that it offers so much about priesthood in a single volume. It's a God-send to the undernourished retreatant in that it provides him with a retreat between covers. It's a source of inspiration to which he can return again and again. Indeed *Our Hide and Seek God* is a book that has considerable value for a very wide readership for reasons that I'll briefly explain.

First of all this is a very pertinent book. It helps to bring Old and New Testament into our age. It sees the word of God primarily in terms of relevance. It analyses that word with thoroughness and scholarship and relates it most effectively to the realities of the present day. Moses for instance having moved out of Egypt and reached the Promised Land is not allowed to stop there. He strides resolutely and relevantly into our time. In his helpful introduction, Fr Neary describes his book as an attempt 'to give expression to a dialogue between God's word and the lived experience of priesthood'.

The dialogue takes place. The author's objective is realised. Rarely have I seen the parallels so carefully drawn between scriptural situations and our own.

Another admirable feature of the book is the clarity of its structure. Fr Neary knows exactly from where he is coming and where it is he wants to go. The themes are explored with authority and expounded with conviction.

In the sections which deal with Adam, Moses and Elijah for instance, he begins with an analysis of God's word, continues with its application to the present day and concludes in summary with an appropriate psalm. The neatness of structure however does not make for pat answers. The impression is not of a subject sealed and set aside. Disturbing questions are asked. Provocative issues raised. Although this book is very encouraging of the priest, it is extremely challenging as well. Faced with the incisiveness of God's word and the insights of the author the reader is invited to respond.

A third feature of this book which will commend itself to readers is the lucidity of its style. This lucidity owes something to the origins of the book in a preached retreat. It owes more, in my view, to the author's grasp of his subject and his ability to communicate. This book is not just reflective and spiritual. It is readable as well. The first chapter alone on 'Silence and Sensitivity' provides sufficient evidence of that.

I congratulate Fr Neary on his achievement. Indeed I celebrate it with him in that he's a priest of the Archdiocese of Tuam. I recommend his book most warmly. I hope, in the general interest of readers, that it is very widely read.

+ JOSEPH CASSIDY, D.D.
ARCHBISHOP OF TUAM

Introduction

In my responsibility of teaching scripture my work is spent analyzing the sacred texts, reading the major works written about those texts and communicating the results to students. This is a most exciting, even though exacting, profession. In recent years I have been invited to preach priests' retreats in a number of dioceses, an experience which I have found invaluable in many ways. These men who have been breaking the bread of God's word Sunday after Sunday for their people have invited, encouraged, and in some cases even pressurized me into publishing the thoughts I shared with them. Fear of the Bible has caused many priests to accuse exegetes of having 'taken away my Lord, and I do not know where they have laid him' (John 20:13)! They are anxious to acquire a competence and confidence in dealing with the word of God which will avoid the fundamentalism of television preachers as well as the facile and superficial approach dictated by feeling and emotion. In the following pages I have attempted to give expression to a dialogue between God's word and the lived experience of priesthood. I have selected certain events and particular biblical personalities for that purpose. Because of the tendency, psychologically understandable but theologically unacceptable, to avoid the Old Testament, I have chosen to range over both Old and New Testaments.

The psalms reflect the mood of the people in times of elation and depression, in situations of faith and fear over a period of about seven hundred years. They directly depict the relationship between the people of God and the people's God. In them we catch glimpses of people both in situations of regression where the raw hurt of the human soul surfaces, and in moments of ecstatic joy. They dismantle the neat systems and rationalizations, creating in the human heart a recognition of honest helplessness which is a prerequisite for the gospel of grace. Jesus quoted more frequently from the psalter than from any other part of the Old Testament. The psalms provide us with a cross-section of the entire Bible. Though we might consider them distant, composed in a culture, mentality and world which is very different, the psalms are prayers with which we can readily identify, in which we can read our own experiences, and through which we can understand and interpret ourselves. For that reason I intend to sum up the sentiments of most of the chapters by a reflection on an appropriate psalm.

I have attempted to combine scholarship with meditation in the hope that a reflective understanding will be born of the alliance; but the reader is the only judge of that. The written word does not convey the resonances of the voice, its intonation, emphasis, emotion, and the immediate warmth of oral communication. Therefore my hope would be that this book be read in a context of prayer, in keeping with the character of a retreat, in a spirit of reflection and openness to contemplation.

Given the history of this book, it is often difficult to retrace just exactly where I first encountered some particularly suggestive line of thought, but I have attempted to give credit to my sources in the course of this work. Informed readers will recognize my dependence on Luis Alonso Schökel and Carlo Martini two of my former professors at the Pontifical Biblical Institute, Rome.

I wish to express my sincere gratitude to the Most Reverend Joseph Cassidy, Archbishop of Tuam, not just for casting a critical eye over the final version, but also for his continued support, inspiration and encouragement of my efforts. I would also like to thank the former Archbishop, the Most Reverend Joseph Cunnane, for enabling me to pursue postgraduate studies. I am indebted to my former professors at St Patrick's College, Maynooth and particularly to my colleagues in the Scripture Department, the Right Reverend Monsignor Seán Quinlan, Rev. Martin Drennan and Rev.

Maurice Hogan SSC. Finally, I wish to thank the Mercier Press for taking the immediate initiative in inviting me to publish.

MICHAEL NEARY
ST. PATRICK'S COLLEGE
MAYNOOTH

1

Silence and Sensitivity

We bring confused emotions with us into a retreat. On the one hand there is the feeling of hope, realizing that we have got away from it all and can relate to, and relax with, the Lord. It is a time when the burden of representation may be left aside for a few days and we can be ourselves. On the other hand there are deep-seated fears within us, fears of what we might discover about ourselves, the fear of having our eyes opened, of having to do a rethink and undertake a readjustment, the fear which comes from asking ourselves a few difficult questions and endeavouring to answer them honestly.

Silence is something which may be relaxing, causing us to feel at home with ourselves and others, or it may be tense, nervous, and uneasy. As men who are ministers of God's word we have invested heavily in verbal communication. Any genuine communication however, needs periods of silence. A retreat is one such occasion. It is significant that many of the things which had been de-emphasized or neglected are being rediscovered today as having immense value.

God gives us many gifts and ministers to us through them. Silence is one such. It is as important as verbal communication and ensures that the latter conveys meaning. Silence is really the space between the letters and the words so that people might have understanding. The notes of music make their greatest impression against a background of silence. For that reason people pay such high prices for reliable stereo equipment so that they may have silence with no interference as the background for appreciating the music that moves them.

God told the Psalmist 'be still and know that I am God' (Ps 46:10). Silence is the medium by which our memory is activated. The past comes back to us when we become still. Our memories bring to our consciousness our past deeds, accomplishments and failures as well as the old wounds, the fears, regrets, lost opportunities, and the successes. As the memory brings the past to mind we begin to detect the thread of God's providence. As the twists and turns of former times are remembered and recalled we begin to notice where and how God has been guiding us. In silent reflection the pattern which God has been working and weaving in our lives becomes apparent, leading us to praise and rejoicing on the one hand and to repentance on the other. As we reflect on the past we become aware of all those things for which we need forgiveness. We are reminded of our broken promises and our betrayed trusts, our greeds and longings, our lack of courtesy, regard and respect for others, when we were heedless of the hurt we have done. It is only when we have faced up to rather than run from that past, and given it to God's grace and mercy that we may find true peace. Silence then, by giving us the opportunity to exercise memory creatively and constructively, in fact ministers to us in a healing fashion.

Silence becomes the language of the soul faced with the mysteries of God. It serves to make us conscious of our Creator and our creaturehood, our destiny and our dependency. Silence becomes a mark of poise and confidence and trust in God. 'In the beginning was the Word' (John 1:1). If our salvation started to become a reality when the word of God dwelt among us it is clear that there must be silence on our part, a silence which is capable of listening, accepting, and allowing God to speak. While our response to the word which manifests itself will be expressed in words of adoration, thanksgiving, and supplication, the primary response to the word will be one of wonder and this must first be expressed in silence. Listening is not complete in the simple act of attending to the proclamation. It must be prolonged by the memory which recalls, reflects, co-ordinates, comprehends and finally discovers the relevance of God's word to my life as a priest.

The ability to live with some interior silence is a mark of the true believer and helps to distance us from the world of incredulity so that we learn to stand back from ourselves and from the events around us to get a more objective view of what is really at stake. What is taking place within me? The answer to that question cannot simply be given in terms of the news media. It is so easy, and psychologically understandable, to shunt the Gospel into the sidings while we become preoccupied with and obsessed by the secular traffic that roars across the main lines of the world.We look on Christ as our refuge for this life and our hope for the next, but do we behave as if the only real force at work in our world is that which determines the events which shuttle across the television screen? The dictates of the dominant culture cannot come to terms with silence. Like Jesus, who at dawn used to go alone to the mountain top to pray and reflect, we too need to have some personal space immune from every alienating din where we may listen attentively to the Father's voice. Our silence ought to be a true silence, filled with God's presence and resounding with his word.

The silent mystery of Mary the mother of God has a special meaning for us. The Gospels contain very few words spoken by her, yet Luke presents her as one who first of all listens, then decides and finally acts. She mirrors the basic human attitude in her openness and submission to truth as a hearer of the word. Mary's silence teaches us how to remain at our present task without wishing it away or escaping into evasive plans for the future and the far away. Like her, we too need to live through and embrace God's silence. Let us ask God therefore to seat us, to settle and silence us and help us to relax so that by mysteries and memories and mastery we may learn to live in faith and trust and to celebrate and enjoy the gifts we have received.

2

Adam and Accountability

All of us have our defence mechanisms and as we get older we become more dependent on them and more adept at using them. Because we have responsibility for preaching salvation we run the risk of speaking and teaching about it objectively, as something out there, something which has taken place in the past. In our reading and explanation of the scriptures there is the great temptation to focus on what a particular passage *meant* in the past rather than what it *means* today.

Creation as Covenant

The story of the exodus from Egypt dominates the Old Testament. It becomes a paradigm in which other stories of rescue from ruin are interpreted. God *chose* a people, *placed* them in a gifted situation in the promised land, *made certain demands* of them (what we call the decalogue), and when they *disobeyed* they were *punished* by means of exile, but having repented they were restored.[1] The stories of creation and fall in the early chapters of the Book of Genesis are written against the background of Israel's history and particularly the exodus experience. We have wasted so much time and energy in the past discussing whether there was an historical Adam or Eve that the real truth of the story has been overlooked. These chapters are misinterpreted if we regard them as speaking of a time lost in the mists of history at the very dawn of creation. In fact these chapters contain parables about our own situation today. We can, without any difficulty, situate ourselves in the story. Reading these pages of Genesis, Adam and Eve, Cain and Abel, the builders of Babel, is equivalent to looking into a mirror. Their reactions are ours.

As priests, we too, like Adam and Eve or Israel, have been *chosen* by God. His initiative and choice has assigned us a special privilege. We are spokesmen for God, reminders of the Lord to others. At our word Christ becomes present in the Eucharist. As was the case for Adam and Eve, so for us there is an *obligation* which is linked to the gift and can only be properly understood in the context of the gift. In their case – not to eat of the forbidden fruit – in our case to live as true ministers of Jesus Christ. In the Genesis story we witness *disobedience*, human rebellion in the form of pride. This finds an echo within each of us. In our case the rebellion may take many forms – basically it is a refusal to allow ourselves to be instruments of God's salvation in the world. In the story of the expulsion from the garden, we witness the *punishment* of Adam and Eve. God's punishment has a purifying purpose, calculated to evoke repentance and return.[2] As priests we may have not been expelled from any garden but I believe we are living through an *exile* situation which I hope to examine in chapter five.

A God Who Asks Questions

Reading chapters one and two of Genesis we get an unmistakable impression of total harmony, complete absence of sin, shame and disorder. It is an idyllic situation, God and man in harmony, man and woman living in confidence and trust with each other and with God's creatures. Then in chapter three another figure enters the story – the serpent. The serpent is the *alter ego* of man through which man's pride and doubts are echoed. The weapon of this animal is the false oracle. By means of a question the seeds of doubt and confusion are sown: 'did God say "you shall not eat of any tree of the garden"?' (Genesis 3:2).

We witness the familiar chain reaction; untruth gathers

momentum. The result is that the divine command is seen to be arbitrary and absurd. The truth of God's command is now distorted, exaggerated, twisted and ultimately denied. After the fall a reversal of creation takes place. In contrast to the intimacy and openness between man and God in chapter two, now man hides from God.

The question God addressed to Adam: 'where are you?' (Genesis 3:9) is the question which he addresses to each of us. The concise dialogue between God and man in Genesis chapter three reveals the confusion, darkness and shame of sin. 'Where are you?' 'Who told you that you were naked?' 'Have you eaten of the tree of which I commanded you not to eat?' We have to deal with a God who asks questions rather than a God who supplies all the answers. Why? In answering the question we ourselves become involved. The question serves to set up a relationship and in that relationship we discover the truth. Our hide and seek God will leave no stone unturned – rather he has left no stone unturned – not even the stone at the empty tomb. He will ransack the wilderness. Samuel he will arouse from his night slumber, Saul of Tarsus will be met on the Damascus road at noon. He will find Isaiah in the temple and Elijah crouching in his cave. The question is where does he find each of us now? We too may have gone into hiding. We may be on the run – endeavouring to escape from ourselves. There is the fear of discovering the real me, where I am at. The joy and exuberance which characterised my relationship with God may have been dimmed. Are there areas of priesthood which have become choked by thickets of one kind or another and which provide me with a defence mechanism in my relationship with God?

Fear and Frustration

In the Genesis narrative social relationships begin to disintegrate with the advent of sin. The mutual trust between man and woman disappears and is replaced by anxiety, uncertainty, fear, frustration, and secrecy. Someone described anxiety as fear without a cause. It stems from a feeling of helplessness, that we are up against forces with which we cannot cope. One of the most crippling and destructive emotions we experience as priests is fear. Fear of what God may in fact be calling us to do, fear of having that question 'where are you?' addressed to us. Then there is the fear of others, the fear of appearing different, strange or innovative; fear of being derided and the fear of freely and courageously proclaiming the gospel message from our heart. How will people react if I preach God's word on justice, chastity, marital fidelity, violence, and respect for the life of the unborn? As priests we may feel threatened by different groups because they make demands of us. Adult religious education groups are anxious to acquire a better understanding of their faith. Many priests feel ill at ease in this situation. As priests we have played down our teaching role. Of course we accept responsibility for preaching, but teaching is something we tend to regard as the responsibility of those in schools and colleges. The Gospel of St Matthew however casts Jesus in a very central role as teacher and the last words of Jesus in that Gospel serve as a key to interpret the whole Gospel. These words place a very powerful emphasis on the teaching responsibility of the disciples: 'go therefore and make disciples of all nations, baptising them in the name of the Father and of the Son, and of the Holy Spirit, *teaching them to observe all that I have commanded you* and lo, I am with you always, to the close of the age' (Matthew 28:19-20).

Fear causes people to react hastily and invariably to overreact. It leads to frustration and secretiveness. We experience this in our own situation and we witness the drama played out in the Genesis narrative. In our own experience we can discern the various ways in which we try to come to terms with fear. There is the ostrich technique. Pretend you are not anxious, present a brave front to the world, bury your head in the sand and hope that your fear will vanish. But do not be surprised should it surface in some other way. Then there is the geographical cure. Say to yourself: 'I am unhappy here, I will move to another appointment. I will leave my fear and anxiety behind me'. Will you? Change may be good for us. But perhaps all we will succeed in doing is taking our anxiety along with us, only to unpack it in our new surroundings. One of the most common techniques of coping with fear is to find the scapegoat. In the Genesis story God's question 'where are you?' brings man to discover the true cause of his fear, namely, the transgression, man's mistaken initiative. Notice the way Adam copes with his fear. Are we any different? In the story we witness the common buck-passing routine as Adam tries to divest himself of blame by locating the blame on Eve, which is a way of imputing ultimate re sponsibility to God himself who gave him the woman as a partner. She passes on the blame to the serpent, one of God's creations, which is an implied fault-finding with the Creator. Both Adam and Eve imply that it is God who has placed them in this sinful environment – a very modern accusation and yet so ancient! We refuse to accept responsibility for our situations. We fail to seize the opportunity provided by an imperfect world and we choose the way of escape through complaints and excuses. Oppositions blame governments, governments blame trade-unions. Priests blame the seminary, their theology, and the formation they received. Students blame their teachers. At all costs keep the heat off ourselves. That shirking of responsibility is one of the effects of sin within ourselves and in the world around us, serving to underline how sin dissociates and separates us from God and from our fellow creatures.

Man's Mistaken Initiatives

As we move into chapter four of Genesis we witness the tragic effects of sin in Cain and Abel. Cain a tiller of the ground and Abel a keeper of sheep – shades of *Oklahoma* – the farmer and the cowboy. Hatred born of envy disrupts the initial brotherhood of men. That story has a particular relevance for the priest. Cain and Abel are offering their produce to the Lord in a religious ceremony. The priest has a particular responsibility for the true worship of God. This story is a very vivid reminder of the need for purification of purpose if we are to worship in spirit and in truth. Envy still impinges on and impedes such worship.

The episode of the building of the tower of Babel in Genesis chapter eleven is the means by which the author expresses human ambition: 'Let us make a name for ourselves' (Genesis 11:4). *Name* is a synonym for *fame*, a name that attracts attention and recognition. The construction of the tower is a manifestation of immeasurable ambition and collective pride, an indication of desire for excessive power and an attempt at a universal domination of God. This is the way of the world – to look for immortality on earth. People want to demonstrate their greatness in a work of their own hands. By contrast with the hectic activity of the constructors of the tower the intervention of God contains very little action. The narrative simply states that God sees, reflects, decides, intervenes, and we witness the effect of his intervention. This story taken in conjunction with the narrative of the fall emphasizes the difficulty we have in allowing God to be and remain God, and the corresponding difficulty in accepting our own creaturehood and limitations.

God's Graceful Initiative

The call of Abraham in chapter twelve is strictly related to the gigantic undertaking of Babel. There is an obvious opposition between the constructors of the tower of Babel who wish to make a *name* for themselves with their own strength, independently of God, and the patriarch Abraham to whom God himself says: 'I will make your *name* great' (Genesis 12:2). The availability of Abraham contrasts sharply with the hiding and refusal of responsibility on the part of Adam. The primeval history is a powerful reminder of how things go wrong when humans take the initiative; mankind tends to destroy what God has made good. The addition of the divine promise (Genesis 12) to the divine command (Genesis 1) counteracts that tendency.

We have to take soundings as priests from time to time.

These chapters of Genesis, which are shot through with forceful insights into human psychology, provide an invaluable support for the taking of such soundings. We can make all sorts of excuses for failing to ask the fundamental questions. We may be so busy and preoccupied that we fail to take cognizance of directions which are emerging or failing to emerge in our lives. What are our main gripes, our particular prejudices? At whom do we point an accusing finger, where do we locate the blame? As priests are we eating forbidden fruit and enabling others to do so? Are we feeding the flock with the word of God or are we providing them with a diet of secularism which promises much but demands little? Are we sufficient reminders of God to our people? Or, are we builders of Babel, taking initiatives independently of God, making names for ourselves, building monuments to ourselves while the name of God is allowed to vanish?

Priests are confronted with the temptation to flee from responsibility, the fear of making a decision and facing the problems of life. It is the temptation to flee from the real, to close one's eyes, hide oneself, pretend to hear and see nothing lest we get involved. How easy it is to compromise, to water down the Gospel message to make it an easy sell. In a permissive age it is easier to hedge one's bets on social and moral issues, to condone rather than condemn. Jesus' exhortation to pray that we do not enter into temptation is a prayer that we do not enter into a comfortable compromise of cowardice, of flight from responsibility. Is my prayer a flight from fear and responsibility or is it a courageous contemplation of what God is asking of me?

The Protective Presence of God

Psalm 139, one of the most penetrating reflections on the meaning of the presence of God in all of literature, captures the sentiments of our reflection on these opening chapters of the bible. The psalmist ponders in a very prayerful way on his life experience which he sees as lived under the protective presence of God who has always kept him in view. Reading the psalm one cannot fail to notice that the focus is on God who is the subject of the majority of the verbs. The psalmist and we ourselves are the object of God's search. The poem opens with an intense celebration of divine knowledge:

O Lord, you search me and you know me,
You know my resting and my rising,
You discern my purpose from afar,
You mark when I walk or lie down,
all my ways lie open to you (v. 1-3).

The omniscience, omnipresence and omnipotence of God are expressed in personalist categories 'I-you' rather than in abstract philosophical terms. Whether resting or rising, human life in its entirety is controlled by God, our thoughts, words and way of life are open to him (v.1-6). Man is enveloped by the protective presence of God:

Behind and before you besiege me
your hand ever laid upon me.

To illustrate this the psalmist explores the spatial dimensions of the universe, height, depth, east and west:

If I climb the heavens, you are there
If I lie in the grave, you are there
If I take the wings of the dawn
and dwell at the sea's furthest end
even there your hand would lead me,
your right hand hold me fast (v. 8-10).

The alternating temporal cycles of day and night are traversed by God and so provide no possibility of escape from him (v.9-12). The absolute beginnings of our existence in the darkness of the womb are an open page to God. Recognizing this, man can only respond with a sense of wonder and awe:

Too wonderful for me, this knowledge,
too high, beyond my reach (v.6).

In his illusory flight from God man discovers that he is
continuously pursued by God. When confronted by the
mysterious love of God, man can only conclude: 'I must be
eternal, like you' (v.18). We are reminded of Psalm 8:

What is man that you should keep him in mind,
mortal man that you care for him?

and also of Sophocles' *Antigone:*

Many are the wonders of the world,
but the greatest of these is man.

Man must remember that this God who is so close to him and
penetrates all secrets cannot remain indifferent in the face of
injustice and must intervene against the ungodly and bring
about the salvation of the just (v. 19-24).

Psalm 139

O Lord, you search me and you know me
you know my resting and my rising,
you discern my purpose from afar.
You mark when I walk or lie down,
all my ways lie open to you.

Before ever a word is on my tongue
you know it, O Lord, through and through.
Behind and before you besiege me,
your hand ever laid upon me.
Too wonderful for me, this knowledge,
too high, beyond my reach.

O where can I go from your spirit,
or where can I flee from your face?
If I climb the heavens, you are there.
If I lie in the grave, you are there.

If I take the wings of the dawn
and dwell at the sea's furthest end,
even there your hand would lead me,
your right hand would hold me fast.

If I say: 'Let the darkness hide me
and the light around me be night,'
even darkness is not dark for you
and the night is as clear as the day.

For it was you who created my being,
knit me together in my mother's womb.
I thank you for the wonder of my being,
for the wonders of all your creation.

Already you know my soul,
my body held no secret from you
when I was being fashioned in secret
and moulded in the depths of the earth.

Your eyes saw all my actions,
they were all of them written in your book;
every one of my days was decreed
before one of them came into being.

To me, how mysterious your thoughts,
the sum of them not to be numbered!
If I count them, they are more than the sand;
to finish, I must be eternal, like you.

O God, that you would slay the wicked!
Men of blood, keep far away from me!
With deceit they rebel against you
and set your designs at naught.

Do I not hate those who hate you,
abhor those who rise against you?
I hate them with a perfect hate
and they are foes to me.

O search me, God, and know my heart.
O test me and know my thoughts.
See that I follow not the wrong path
and lead me in the path of life eternal.

3

Moses: Energy and Enthusiasm

In bringing us to salvation God provides us with leaders who become mediators. Moses is one such as he leads God's people out of Egypt and interprets events for them. In that task of leading and interpreting, the priest, like Moses, is faced with opposition and hostility not only on the part of those who perpetrate the oppression but also on the part of the oppressed whom he wishes to liberate. In the speech which he places on the lips of Stephen in the Acts of the Apostles, Luke detects three stages in the life of the great mediator (Acts 7:20-36).[3] Firstly his time in Egypt when, shortly after his birth, Moses was abandoned and adopted by the Pharaoh's daughter where he 'was instructed in all the wisdom of the Egyptians and he was mighty in his words and deeds' (Acts 7:22). Like Moses the priest is one chosen for a delicate task. Word and deed serve to express the ministry of the priest. During his Egyptian training Moses would have been introduced to the best methodologies and the most persuasive diplomacy. He becomes impatient and is anxious to apply the answers which he thinks he has. He approaches reality through the ideologies which he has acquired. He considers that he has his finger on the pulse but fails to appreciate the distance between reality and its image. A great temptation facing the priest is to approach life in terms of problems which require solution.

Moses, Enslaved by an Ideology

The second stage in Moses' life commences when he endeavours to apply the Egyptian wisdom to an oppressed people. This stage, determined by generosity on his part, ends in violence, frustration, and exile. He murders an Egyptian who was maltreating a Hebrew and then proceeds to settle a dispute between two Hebrews and reconcile those at loggerheads while defending the innocent. He has no option but to flee the country. In Midian he cannot restrain from fighting oppression and intervenes on the weaker side when he witnesses Jethro's daughters being bullied by the shepherds. Moses is a man with a consuming desire for justice and fair play, but one whose emotions can easily run away with him and involve him in trouble. His struggle for justice leads him to violence. Furnishing his brothers with a sense of dignity and unity had been uppermost in his mind and to this end he considered they must have freedom imposed on them. The great liberator however failed to take seriously the opposition of the oppressed in their desire for freedom: 'He supposed that his brethren understood that God was giving them deliverance by his hand, *but they did not understand*' (Acts 7:25). This comment gives us an appreciation of the real resistance which leads to the rejection of the prophet: 'who has made you a ruler and judge over us?' (Acts 7:27).

How often do we in our priesthood encounter similar situations, convinced of the solutions which we feel society sorely needs, only to find ourselves ridiculed and rejected? There is a form of false practicality where we allow ourselves to be guided by an ideology in which we bend our experience to suit an arbitrary idea of reality and in its name we neglect the attentiveness due to people and situations around us. Moses had assumed the mantle of saviour and judge but when the people fail to move forward at his pace the liberator can no longer cope. He is impulsive to the point of violence. The courageous prophet has to flee the country after the murder of the Egyptian: 'He became an exile in the land of Midian, where he became the father of two sons' (Acts 7:29).

He has become totally disillusioned with his liberation theology and the methodologies which he had acquired at the Egyptian court. What is the point of it all, he says to himself, why not settle down, live as a private citizen and tend to my own affairs? How often when things fail to go according to our plans and we experience rejection do we retreat into the Midian of our mental exile. On occasions like this we should ask ourselves a serious question: who was being served during this time; was it the cause of God or was it myself? Who was Moses serving at that stage? The great prophet has to learn in a very painful way the truth that liberation or salvation will not come from brutal power but from gentle love.

In our own experience we can identify with Moses. God creates desert situations for us in order to liberate us from our idols and ideologies. This may take the form of rejection by someone, tribulation, failure, and disillusionment. There may be a history of confusion, of self-doubt, of interior anguish as we have to deal with fear, come to terms with frustrations, and accept deflated expectations. This liability to suffering constitutes a critically important indication of the call of God as our hierarchy of values is revealed and our attachment whether to ourselves, to our ability and achievement, or to our plans and programmes becomes exposed. As supports and defences disappear, in our vulnerability, like Moses, we become more sensitive and responsive to the call of God.

Moses, Liberated by God's Call

The third and final stage in the life of the liberator commences when the prophet becomes conscious of his role as God's instrument in the work of liberation. He had become a shepherd far away from the glamour of Pharaoh's court. As the years roll on the memories begin to fade. Yet his thoughts kept pursuing him. He could not forget the slave gangs, the crack of the whip, and the sharp shrill cry of pain. Moses had the training for leadership yet he had abandoned his oppressed compatriots. God now takes the initiative. The prophet recognizes that God was seeking him, and to his everlasting wonder, he finds that God is interested in the very things which Moses had been so passionately pursuing. He is astonished to hear that God is commissioning him for this divine work.

The extended dialogue in chapters three and four of Exodus which narrates the call and mission of Moses serves to underline a central point: the liberation which is about to take place will be God's work and not a human achievement. Scholars have acknowledged that the call of the liberator is presented in the categories of the prophetic call form. We can detect different elements. Firstly there is the divine confrontation which takes place at a time of crisis for the Israelites in Egypt. Moses was going about his ordinary business of minding sheep, so it is not an ecstatic experience. It is however a disruptive one indicating that Moses will have to return to the Egypt from which he had fled. In the second part of the call form we find the introductory word which establishes an intimate relationship with God, creating in Moses a receptivity to the word and work of God. The two-fold address 'Moses, Moses' in Exodus 3:4 testifies to the solemnity of the moment of revelation. Thirdly Moses is commissioned as one sent by God, 'come, I will send you to Pharaoh that you may bring forth my people, the sons of Israel, out of Egypt' (Exodus 3:10). Moses twisted and turned to evade the call of God. His objections are outlined on five occasions and we must surely be able to identify with him at this point: 'Who am I that should go to Pharaoh and bring the sons of Israel out of Egypt?' (3:11). He is humanly ill-equipped to accomplish such a task. Surely God has known that he had been a fugitive from Egyptian justice and an outcast from his own people. The prophet's objection does not cut any ice with God. Moses is reassured that the efficacious presence of God removes all grounds for objection or hesitation: 'But I will be with you' (3:12). In the eyes of the people Moses will be vindicated when they worship God: 'this shall be the sign for you that I have sent you: when you have brought forth the people out of Egypt, you shall serve God upon this mountain' (3:12). Because the sign does not happen immediately it demands the faith and obedience of Moses. By worshipping God the Israelites will become conscious of their liberation and Moses will recognize the validity of his mission. The use of this call form interprets the role of Moses and indicates that the liberator participates in the plan of God.

To this personal call Moses responds knowingly and consciously 'here I am' (3:4). Having presented himself God reveals his plan of salvation. He has seen, he has heard, he knows and is now going to intervene: 'I have seen the ill-treatment of my people that are in Egypt and heard their groaning, and I have come down to deliver them' (3:7-8). The plan of salvation is unfolded in the mission of Moses. There are two key verbs in Exodus 3:10, 'I will *send* you to Pharaoh that you may *lead forth* my people, the sons of Israel, out of Egypt'. The active subject of the second verb is Moses, sent by God and acting in his name. Although he had declared his availability for his mission the prophet still manufactures and multiplies obstacles and excuses. He asks God to identify himself only to receive the mysterious name 'I am' (3:13-14). The prophet is frightened by the possibility of failure, in view of the obstinacy of the people: 'they will not believe me or listen to my voice' (4:1-2), to which God responds by presenting the liberator as a wonder-worker, whose miracles will authenticate his mission. When he declares his personal inadequacy as a communicator God provides Aaron (4:10-17). Moses acknowledges that someone must be sent and is happy if that someone is not himself: 'Oh, my Lord, send I pray, some other person' (4:13). So the prophet somewhat reluctantly retraces his steps to Egypt invested with a God-given mission, in spite of a terrible sinking sense of incapacity.

Idealism Transformed by Grace

Moses is under no illusion as to the enormity of the task facing him. In his previous attempt he had failed miserably when resorting to force. His approach on this occasion is determined by the *word*; 'you shall *say* to Pharaoh . . .' (Exodus 4:22). The prophet is now confident in the power of God's word although the circumstances are not conducive to liberation, and Pharaoh is stubborn. Moses' role will be an instrumental and important one but the action will be decisively divine. This discovery enables the former fugitive to accept his past failures; he no longer places a premium on himself. There is no need to be obsessed with or discouraged by the reaction and rejection of his own people. He can now cope with their resistance. The shortcomings of his previous approach have become obvious. He had longed to liberate the people within the limits and imperfections of his impulsive character, but now God yearns within the infinite depths of his holiness. Moses had struck a futile blow with his own hand but now God promises to display the power of his own mighty arm which alone can effectively deliver people from bondage. The prophet's previous approach of coercive power would not really produce freedom; it would merely replace one tyrant with another as the oppressed became the new oppressor. Moses begins to understand that his own idealism and energy are insufficient, only God can genuinely set men and women free and now he takes Moses into his plan of campaign to liberate his people. The sun of God's promise meets the sea of God's possibilities and things now begin to come together for the prophet and, as he starts to respond to the divine initiative, his idealism is transformed by God's grace. At this point the mission of Moses can begin in earnest.

In which of these three stages of the life of Moses do I find myself? Am I in the first stage, picking up the methodologies, becoming enslaved by ideologies, dealing with plans and problems rather than with people? Or, in one of the expressions that has filtered through from Hippieland, am I doing my own thing, like Moses in Midian? Or do I find myself in that third stage, recognizing that God is interested in the very same concerns which occupy me, but the initiative lies with him and I must tune in to his initiative? What emotions characterize my living of priesthood – joy, euphoria and enthusiasm, or self-pity, tiredness and resignation?

Human Resistance to Liberation

Liberation involves loss of security of a kind. In our own experience we are afraid to risk liberty lest we lose our security. Adventure and risk are involved. Return to Egypt and its flesh-pots is a perennial temptation. People, if deprived of hope, will readily resort either to violence or materialism. This happens in the Exodus narrative. Moses insists that freedom, properly understood, must find expression in the service of God. The journey is one from *slavery* in Egypt to *service* of God and in the original Hebrew there is a very definite play on these words. 'Let my people go, that they may hold a feast to me in the wilderness' (Exodus 5:1). The response of Pharaoh is that of a political pragmatist of considerable diplomatic skill. The interests of the oppressor do not recognize the rights of the oppressed nor are they disposed to cease in their exploitation. Pharaoh accordingly identifies worship with laziness. It is not productive, it takes people away from their work.[4] Worship however, properly interpreted, is both an experience and expression of liberty. Our modern consumerist society is in great danger of overlooking that fact. We witness the Pharaoh's attitude in the approach to Sabbath observance.[5] Pharaoh is not free, cannot allow change, and feels threatened and uneasy by a demand for it. He has become conditioned to a position of privilege and will not have his social status challenged or changed. Is there not something of Pharaoh in all of us? We tend to get the balance so wrong between work and worship. It is so easy to become cushioned and conditioned; pragmatism and prejudice may dominate as power and prestige take precedence over poverty and principle.

Because Moses is now convinced that God is interested in

the burning issues of unbearable oppression which had provoked an impulsive reaction at an earlier stage, and because he now sees himself as God's instrument he can confront the Pharaoh patiently while insisting tenaciously on God's demand for the liberation of the oppressed. Courage has replaced caution and cowardice. He passionately believes in the power of God's word in spite of the obduracy of the Egyptian. Have we as priests given up too easily at the first signs of opposition or rejection when we attempted to challenge both oppressor and oppressed? The prophet has to cope with the resistance of those who are being liberated They hope for instant success but when the Pharaoh remains obstinate the oppression intensifies and the people rebel against Moses declaring that his intervention brings death (5:21-22). In our own ministry we will have experienced similar opposition from those whom we had hoped to serve and to liberate. Freedom involves risk and it is only won and defended amidst dangers. In the human heart there is a tension between the desire for liberty and a desire for security. There is the fear to take the necessary risk in freedom because it may involve loss of security. In the Exodus narrative the wilderness wandering is situated between the going out from Egypt and the entry to the promised land. The desert is a time of waiting and purification. The hope and active perseverance which should characterize such a time is frequently obscured by a reluctance to be led and by misunderstanding. This is very true in our situation today which calls for instant success and cannot cope with the rugged or routine. The protest of the Israelites contains a value judgment, namely, slavery with nourishment in Egypt was better than want in the wilderness, and so the whole meaning of the exodus is distorted (15:2-3). There is a great temptation to defend oneself in such a hostile climate but the qualities demanded whether of Moses or of the priest are natural prudence, sincerity in relation to others, disinterestedness and fear of the Lord: 'Men... such as fear God, men who are trustworthy and who hate a bribe' (18:21). We can sympathize with Moses as he finds himself placed between the people and God. His identification with the people is un-questioned. After the golden calf incident he addressed God: 'if thou wilt forgive their sin – if not, blot me I pray, out of thy book which thou hast written' (Exodus 32:32). The mediator, whether then or now, must endure all the anguish of situations to which there is no apparent solution. In this way God calls for faith in the power of his word. At times our identification with people and their problems tends to blur our vision causing us to exacerbate obstacles and leading to lack of faith in God. We become conscious of the gaping discrepancy between our own ability and the enormity of the challenge confronting us. Even Moses yields at one such pressure point. The people are growing impatient by the hour. They refuse to make progress on the way to the promised land. He consents to the people's desire to enter the land by a route leading eastward to the Jordan rather than from the south because they had become discouraged and frightened at the report of the scouts regarding the inhabitants of the land. Moses succumbed at that point and became more conscious of the problems of the people than of the power of God. Because of this failure of nerve and loss of faith the prophet is punished: 'the Lord was angry with me on your account, and he swore that I should not cross the Jordan, and that I should not enter the good land which the Lord your God gives you for an inheritance' (Deuteronomy 4:21). He pays the price for his involvement with the people.

Variety in The Ministry of Moses

In his vocation Moses has to answer the call of God in the various vicissitudes of the life of the people. For the people of the Old Testament the sea was frequently seen as a cosmic threat to mankind. In Exodus chapter 15 we get a simple but very expressive parallelism . The cosmic enemy is placed at the service of the Lord as the sons of Israel pass through while the human enemies, the Egyptians, are overcome. The enthusiasm which greets this work of God is short-lived however, for in the following scenes the people are confronted by the primary necessities of life, the two fundamental threats of the desert, namely thirst (15:23-25) and hunger (16:3). In the solitude of the wilderness they encounter God who teaches the elementary lessons and explains the relationship between hunger and the manna, thirst and the water from the rock. As the man on the spot Moses must take these complaints seriously and ensure that the elementary human needs of the people are satisfied but this kind of service must not be seen as exhausting his vocation. In his exercise of authority the prophet sees himself as judge who must deal with every conceivable problem. Our own experience of being busy can easily convey the impression of indispensability. Moses has to learn from his father-in-law, Jethro, the importance of delegating wisely and differentiating between the important and the trivial, something which we as priests find more difficult than we are prepared to admit. Today the priest is very conscious of the burden of responsibility and representation which he carries. Moses as a realist, accepting the people as they are in their anxiety and anger, addresses them on the subject of his burden and approves of their choice of 'wise, understanding, and experienced men' (Deuteronomy 1:12-13). In this way he learns to live with and exercise responsibility without becoming obsessed by it.

Much of his ministry is taken up with intercession. The prayer of intercession in Israelite literature is very uninhibited, sometimes to the point of shaking a clenched fist at God. The language used is expressive of a raw ruthless honesty, demanding that God treat him just as he does his brothers (as we have seen in the golden calf episode Exodus 32:32). When the people begin to lose hope as they find themselves hemmed in between the Egyptians and the sea, Moses must summon up all his reserves as he faces a chorus of complaint from the sons of Israel: 'what have you done to us. . . let us alone and let us serve the Egyptians. For it would have been better for us to serve the Egyptians than to die in the wilderness?' (Exodus 14:11-12). It is so easy for us to misinterpret and personalize bitter complaint and fail to recognize it as the cry of hopelessness. Moses is a model for us on this occasion as he becomes a minister of consolation. Using the classic form of an oracle of salvation he invites them not to fear, and announcing certain victory, he recommends calm: 'Fear not, stand firm, and see the salvation of the Lord, which he will work for you today; for the Egyptians whom you see today, you shall never see again' (Exodus 14:13).

The Ministry of the Word

While Moses is called upon to provide this varied form of service, the ministry of the word of God is what characterizes his approach. He is God's spokesman, an intermediary of the covenant, and through the trials and solidarity with his people, he achieves a most intimate relationship with God. Because of this Moses can live dangerously. In his search for security he has discovered not that he is interested in God but rather that he himself has been graced by a God who is passionately interested in him. Because of this the prophet becomes a *forth*teller rather than a *fore*teller, and as a bearer of God's word, he can confidently and courageously address the sender and those to whom he is sent. In him the past of God's promise meets the stress of the present and sustains him against the fear of the future. His prophetic ministry, and our priestly one, depends on incredible intimacy with God and a passionate concern for God's people. The task laid upon him would have taxed a master of psychological tactics as he applied his persuasive powers in two different directions; to his own people and to Pharaoh. He had to undertake leadership and responsibility; he must stand firm against and master the churlish behaviour of those to whom he is sent.

Confidence in the Midst of Confusion

The conflicting and confusing sentiments of affliction, anguish and hope which were central to his ministry and to ours may be captured in the words of Psalm 31. That psalm may be subdivided into a psalm of confidence (v.1-8), a hymn of lament with a strong supplication (v.9-18), followed by a hymn of joy (v.19-24). In the poem we catch a glimpse of the emotions and moods of one who, in his deprivation and distress, seeks support in the Lord. The psalmist frankly and fearlessly acknowledges and gives expression to his fluctuating feelings. His prayer is answered as he comes into God's presence and fear yields to faith. As a result the psalmist becomes a beacon of light and hope for others who experience similar sentiments.

In the first section we note the call addressed to God with the aid of the imperatives. 'Hear me', 'rescue me speedily', implying that the psalmist is on the edge of the cliff, 'be a rock of refuge for me', 'lead me and guide me'. The poet recognizes that the only safety in the storm of life comes from communion with God in the temple. The protective hand of God rescues the persecuted. In a spirit of total abandonment to God the psalmist entrusts to him the most precious gift he has – his spirit: 'into your hands I commend my spirit' (v. 5). A protest of innocence follows which has a negative aspect – refutation of idols, and a positive one – trust in the Lord (v.6). This trust anticipates the joy of liberation. Significantly the verbs used to denote the salvific action of God 'thou hast *seen* my affliction; *taken heed*. . . *delivered*' echo the verbs of Exodus 3:7-8 which we have already examined.

The lament section follows the classical form as the distress of the persecuted is highlighted. He has become an object of scorn to his enemies, and is avoided by his friends (v.11-12), the object of a whispering campaign on the part of the unscrupulous (v.13). The poet's thoughts in this situation turn towards trust in God whom he addresses in the second person:

> But as for me, I trust in you, Lord,
> I say you are my God (v. 14)

and from whom alone he can expect steadfast love (*Hesed*)

(v.16). In the hymn (v.19-24) the fullness of happiness which comes from communion with God is celebrated. This happiness is not an exclusive personal possession. Before the congregation he bears witness to God's steadfast love which is the source of the salvation he has experienced.

Psalm 31

In you, O Lord, I take refuge.
Let me never be put to shame.
In your justice, set me free,
hear me and speedily rescue me.

Be a rock of refuge for me,
a mighty stronghold to save me,
for you are my rock, my stronghold.
For your name's sake, lead me and guide me.

Release me from the snares they have hidden
for you are my refuge, Lord.
Into your hands I commend my spirit.
It is you who will redeem me, Lord.

O God of truth, you detest
those who worship false and empty gods.
As for me, I trust in the Lord:
let me be glad and rejoice in your love.

You who have seen my affliction
and taken heed of my soul's distress,
have not handed me over to the enemy,
but set my feet at large.

Have mercy on me, O Lord,
for I am in distress.
Tears have wasted my eyes,
my throat and my heart.

For my life is spent with sorrow
and my years with sighs.
Affliction has broken down my strength

and my bones waste away.

In the face of all my foes
I am a reproach,
an object of scorn to my neighbours
and of fear to my friends.

Those who see me in the street
run far away from me.
I am like a dead man, forgotten in men's hearts,
like a thing thrown away.

I have heard the slander of the crowd,
fear is all around me,
as they plot together against me,
as they plan to take my life.

But as for me, I trust in you, Lord,
I say: 'You are my God.
My life is in your hands, deliver me
from the hands of those who hate me.

Let your face shine on your servant.
Save me in your love.
Let me not be put to shame for I call you,
but let the wicked be put to shame!

Let them be silenced in the grave,
let lying lips be dumb,
that speak haughtily against the just
with pride and contempt.'

How great is the goodness, Lord,
that you keep for those who fear you,
that you show to those who trust you
in the sight of men.

You hide them in the shelter of your presence
from the plotting of men:
you keep them safe within your tent
from disputing tongues.

Blessed be the Lord who has shown me
the wonders of his love
in a fortified city.

'I am far removed from your sight'
I said in my alarm.
Yet you heard the voice of my plea
when I cried for help.

Love the Lord, all you saints.
He guards his faithful
but the Lord will repay to the full
those who act with pride.

Be strong, let your heart take courage,
all who hope in the Lord.

4

Elijah and Exhaustion

After five, fifteen, or fifty years of priesthood it is not easy to stand back and analyse. It has become so much part of our life – the Mass, sacraments, pastoral visitation, celibacy. In this reflection I hope to focus on a scene in the Bible where we catch a glimpse of a man of God struggling to come to some understanding of the mission which he has received. His wrestling with his God and the tempestuous and volcanic nature of his relationship with Him may help us to reflect on and interpret where we now find ourselves in our ministry.

As priests we are inevitably affected by the present climate of opinion which feels free to pick and choose between doctrines, embracing what is distant and not very demanding while dismissing or de-emphasizing what hurts, impinges and is challenging. Belief in the one true God seems capable of being expressed alongside belief in countless other false gods. The surge of a counter-culture threatens to sweep people off their feet. False prophets proliferate, demanding little but promising much. We live in a society which is rapidly losing its taste for risk, for gambling on a future in God, for self-surrender to the Father. Values in which we believed and which have served society so well and for so long are now presented as old-fashioned and outmoded. This situation frequently leaves us scared into silence. Yet deep down we recognize it is an occasion for courage and an opportunity for genuine faith. I invite you therefore to reflect on the reactions of one who experienced those mixed emotions of courage and fear as he endeavoured to remain faithful to his vocation in difficult times, the prophet Elijah. As priests we have experienced success and fulfilment. In our celebration of the liturgy there are times when we ourselves feel uplifted and where we are conscious of picking up others who are downcast and setting them on the road of life again. At times we catch glimpses of success in moments where we consider that we were getting through to difficult people who were beginning to show an interest in religious values. Sometimes the stray Samaritan returns to register appreciation – perhaps after many years. From time to time in the confessional we savour some success as we, or rather the grace of God working through us, enable penitents to disentangle difficult areas of their lives. Success leaves us happy and fulfilled but it is inevitably followed by failure, by questions like 'what am I doing here?' 'What is the point in it all?' 'Where are the tangible results for all my time and the energy invested?' 'Where do I go from here?' Shall I resort to a form of mental exile in which I hold on to my own beliefs but feel no responsibility for confronting the tide of popular opinion and secularism, presenting people with a choice and impressing on them the necessity and urgency to make such?

A Culture of Compromise

To appreciate the task facing Elijah one must have some understanding of the insidious and destructive power of Baalism, a nature religion, which posed a seductive temptation for the Israelites in Canaan. The sociological shift from being a semi-nomadic people to a settled community brought with it corresponding difficulties for the faith. The big temptation is that Israel will forget the Lord and will interpret God's gift of the land as their human achievement. The cult of idols, something absolutely forbidden for the Israelite, is central to the Canaanite system. New and unforeseen demands will be made on Israelite faith if God is not to be manipulated and reduced to the manageable proportions of a fertility deity. In the desert the people had lived exposed and vulnerable; in the land they are at home and secure. The land was rich in productivity and there is the real danger that they will be drawn into the producer-consumer cycle which is a closed system, self-explanatory, and looks on God as part of disposable society. This leads either to complacency and self-indulgent materialism on the one hand or to despair on the other. We might even be speaking of economic prosperity today. The Book of Deuteronomy indicates how the people could resist the temptation, namely, by remembering the Lord and his works. The Torah will ensure that the people do not forget either the Giver or the gift and will be a powerful weapon against reducing the mystery to manageable proportions.

The idealism of the exodus was quickly betrayed however, and the glories of the Davidic kingdom were short-lived. Solomon, David's son and successor, became defensive and oppressive. Religion became massive and monumental and, while affluence did increase, it brought oppressive social policy in its wake. Religion had become a haven of protection for the powerful and privileged but did nothing to alleviate the misery of the many. Superficially this was a period of calm as places of pilgrimage were visited, altars sent up their smoke and religious language and symbolism was used. Beneath the surface however, a gradual erosion of religious values and of faith in God had been taking place almost imperceptibly. False gods had been competing quietly for some time now and their followers had grown in numbers and in confidence. Given the opportune moment of a supportive political regime it was inevitable that things would come to a head. The presence of Ahab on the throne of the Northern Kingdom (869-850 BC), governed by his ambitious and unscrupulous Phoenician wife Jezebel, revealed the alarming extent of Israel's apostasy. Care and concern for the widow, orphan, and resident alien had been central tenets of Israel's religious system. Jezebel represented the seductive influence of pagan religion, so when the powerful Ahab coveted the little vineyard of Naboth it was she who engineered its acquisition. At the royal court and among the upper classes Israel's religious ideals were being seriously compromised. The pagan god Baal now had devoted followers. This is the situation confronting Elijah. The crisis for religious faith was all the more insidious in that the majority of the people did not seem to be aware of the gravity of the situation since they had grown accustomed to accommodation.

Courageous Call for Exclusive Allegiance

The prophet could not remain neutral in the face of this threat of a nature religion with its attendant problems. Compromise, false tolerance, and syncretism were incompatible with the Lord's claim for exclusive allegiance.[6] Elijah appears as a prophetic champion for belief in the one God against pagan rivals.

The stories about him are vivid and dramatic, raising a poor widow's son from the dead, winning a contest on Mount Carmel against the pagan prophets of Baal but then fleeing in fear from the fury of Jezebel. The prophet is portrayed as a man of God who exercises this power in the cause of God, courageously confronting evil and then struggling with the mystery of God in his own ministry. He seems to have been the first prophetic champion for belief in God against pagan rivals. It falls to him to make people alert to the faith crisis of Israel. He confronts them with a crucial either/or decision. They must decide on who was to be God, the Lord or the pagan god Baal.[7] This approach took the prophet's contemporaries by surprise. They had never viewed the situation in the mutually exclusive categories which Elijah had put before them. Accommodation had been acceptable in their eyes; worship of God and pagan devotions coexisted. It is a time for decision rather than diplomacy so the prophet's question is direct: 'How long will you go limping with two different opinions? If the Lord is God, follow him; but if Baal, then follow him' (1 Kings 18:21). The narrative implies that the people reacted in silence: 'they did not answer him a word' (1 Kings 18:21). This probably indicates that the people were taken aback at his approach. Why make such a decision when no one considered it necessary? That choice would not have been familiar to his hearers. The prophet has to make an heroic effort before he succeeds in impressing upon them the importance of making a decision for which they saw no great need. For him the coalescing of two forms of worship in which the people were happy was unacceptable. The First Book of Kings chapter 18 presents this lonely prophetic figure locked in combat with the four hundred and fifty pagan prophets of Baal. The issue centres upon which God has the power to conquer the drought and send the life-giving rain which will lead to prodigious fertility for the land. The writer contrasts the calm composure of Elijah with the frenzy of the pagan prophets.

Despondency and the Death-Wish

After his success on Mount Carmel however, Elijah begins to despair. The extermination of faith in the Lord seems to be the reason for his despondency. He suffers a form of burnout as listlessness and defeatism overtake him. In chapter nineteen we notice that Elijah has fled south to Horeb to escape the persecution of Jezebel. It is a time of national apostasy which threatens the prophet's own vocation. He arrives at Horeb a defeated figure. The extent of his defeat may be measured by the death-wish which he expresses: 'and he asked that he might die, saying, "It is enough: now, O Lord, take away my life" ' (1 Kings 19:4). He retreats to a cave hoping to escape the demands of his vocation, only to hear the Lord addressing him: 'what are you doing here, Elijah?' (1 Kings 19:9). There follows a lengthy reply in which the prophet complains bitterly concerning his fate. He contrasts his own steadfastness with the waywardness of his people, complaining that he alone has been faithful to the Lord, and now he is being sought by those intent on killing him: 'I have been very jealous for the Lord, the God of hosts; for the people of Israel have forsaken thy covenant, thrown down thy altars and slain thy prophets with the sword; and I, even I only, am left; and they seek my life to take it away' (1 Kings 19:10).

Elijah's most grievous complaint is his conviction that the cause of God has been abandoned in Israel. The Lord does not reply directly to this accusation. The prophet must recognize that this is not a time to languish in grief or resort to regret. A whining self-pity is not going to further the cause of God. The Lord sends Elijah out to stand at the mouth of the cave. Immediately after he receives this command, the prophet experiences God, but not in the traditional symbols of his presence, in wind, earthquake, and fire, but rather in a 'still small voice' (1 Kings 19:12), which follows the violent phenomena of wind, earthquake, and fire.

Recommissioning of Elijah

At this point, Elijah at last is addressed by the Lord with the same words as before: 'what are you doing here, Elijah?' (1 Kings 19:13). And the prophet in turn, responds with precisely the same words as before. The odds are against him, he had been zealous for the covenant and had fought the good fight but was now tiring. Although the words of question and reply are exactly the same, a change has taken place in the man who replies to the question. The first time he had spoken these words he was a fugitive. Then he seemed to wallow in self-pity, but now he is defiant and ready to resume his prophetic vocation. This section, like the previous one, concludes with a command which Elijah obeys. The first command [v.11] had sent the prophet to stand at the entrance of the cave to experience the theophany, but this time the command is to continue in his prophetic role: 'go, return on your way to the wilderness of Damascus' (1 Kings 19:15). The narrator uses repetition to create a most powerful effect. The first time the prophet responds to the Lord's questions, his words constitute a bitter lament, complaining that God in effect has let him down, but on the second occasion, precisely the same words are spoken in absolute defiance of all who conspire against the cause of God by one who is ready and willing to perform his God-given task. The change in the prophet's reaction and his response to God's question must be attributed to the fact that on the mountain he has met the Lord, a meeting which has restored his courage.

The story of Elijah is of more than merely historic interest. It is the story of a prophet trapped in the trough of deep depression. He is one like us in our frailties and has that introspective bearing that frequently characterizes the depressed personality. Most of us encounter in our ministry times of disillusionment and despondency. I believe we can cope with these situations more effectively if we can locate their possible origins and the causes which contributed. The real value of 1 Kings 17-19 may be located in the frank exposures of the fluctuating emotions of the prophet. As a man of God he had hoped for a successful service of the Lord, but he is confronted by depression, disillusionment and doubt. One might have thought that Elijah's victory over the prophets of Baal would have put God's power and faithfulness beyond doubt. But high moments of spiritual experience are danger areas since reactions can so easily follow. Achievements can leave one emotionally drained with no reserves on which to call. Matthew and Mark and to a lesser extent Luke, recognize that fact as they present the temptations of Jesus in the wilderness following immediately on his experience of the opened heavens at his baptism.

Elijah was at an emotional low. Nervous and physical exhaustion however only partially account for his state. There were basic weaknesses in his approach to his vocation which render his spiritual collapse more understandable. The narrative attributes his depression to fear which deflates the human spirit leaving it depleted. After his victory on Mount Carmel the prophet felt abandoned by God and ran for cover from the wrath of Jezebel: 'he was afraid, and he arose and went for his life' (1 Kings 19:3). It is difficult to comprehend one of his calibre and courage caught in the grip of fear. In addition to the present alarm there is a memory of disappointment which haunts him. The prophet had sown the seeds of hope in a field of doubt but the harvest is not forthcoming and he does not see the results. On Mount Carmel he had passionately longed for the people's repentance and return to the God of the covenant and had prayed precisely for that intention. However there was no visible national repentance, indeed the political situation seemed to suggest the opposite. When hope is deferred and genuine expectations are not realized our resistance to depression is diminished. In his conflict with the pagan prophets we may detect a certain self-importance in Elijah's prayer as he lays claim to be the sole surviving prophet of the Lord: 'I, even I only, am left a prophet of the Lord' (1 Kings 18:22). This obsessive sense of responsibility is reiterated in 1 Kings 19:10 and 19:14. Overwhelmed and preoccupied with the religious collapse around him he lives under the illusion of being the sole survivor of the faithful and therefore he must bear the burden of defending the true faith and maintaining the rejected values.

The priest today may be tempted to over-react in a similar way to the moral and religious climate in which he finds himself. Elijah felt that the task was too tough, the responsibility too great. This is a form of egocentricity and it leads the prophet down the road of disappointment, humiliation and fear. He seeks the easy way out in his expression of the death-wish. His whole demeanour is marked by self-pity, an insight into which may be gained by his words: 'I am no better than any of my fathers' (1 Kings 19:4). His introspective attitude leads to this false sense of self-esteem and from this imprisoning and depressing egocentricism he cannot extricate himself. In these circumstances it is understandable that exaggeration and lack of balance would characterize his outlook. On Mount Carmel, as we have seen, he declared himself the only surviving defender of God's cause, everything hinges around him and depends on him. In his depressed self-preoccupation he has overlooked the fact that

seven thousand have remained devoted to the God of the
covenant (1 Kings 19:18). The experience of loneliness may
plunge us into bitterness as others fail to live up to our over-
high hopes and demands. Or it may drive us into querulous
self-pity so that we go through life perpetually complaining
about being isolated and misunderstood. Elijah was not
alone in his fidelity to God as he had complained.

To the prophet's despairing cry God responds, 'Go, return
on your way to the wilderness of Damascus' (1 Kings 19:15).
Elijah's work was not yet finished. The experience on Mount
Horeb has taken him from self-pity to renewed courage and
confidence in his mission from the Lord. We witness here the
beginning of his recovery of self-respect. As priests we all
stand in need of some personal word from God, addressed to
us by name. God's call: 'what are you doing here, Elijah?' (1
Kings 19:9,13) was calculated to jolt the prophet and shake
him out of self-centredness and self-pity. The Lord addresses
that question to us 'what are you doing here' in order to open
our eyes and provide us with a recommissioning grace. Like
the prophet we too tend to be burdened by an excessive sense
of responsibility which causes us to become discouraged at
the rejection of God and religious values, the declining
standards and the indifference whether to past or to pre-
cedent or to a future that is foreseeable. Nostalgia is a great
temptation for despairing priests as well as for despairing
prophets. Elijah had received a recommissioning grace which
summoned him back with renewed enthusiasm to his prophetic ministry.

An Unexpected Presence of God

The traditional symbols of God's mysterious presence in the
Old Testament especially in the Exodus traditions, wind,
earthquake and fire, have been emptied and left meaning-
less. Elijah recognized that God was not present in them. But
the Lord was not absent. He was there in a 'still small voice'
in the sound of silence. The unexpected had replaced the
expected and God's puzzling absence was but a prelude to

his surprising presence. The prophet had to discover the still centre which was immune to the pressure of circumstances and unassailed by the constant ebb and flow of the fluctuating emotions. The prophet had not learned to live at the centre of God's peace. His continual confrontation with anti-God forces triggered off an inner turmoil within his heart which undermined his confidence. Memory of former triumphs like the one on Mount Carmel did not allay the fear of the future. God had to show him that the ultimate reality is not to be found in the natural turbulence of wind, earthquake and fire but in the sound of 'a still small voice' (1 Kings 19:12). This is an important lesson for us living as we do in times not unlike that of the prophet. Like him we must discover a faith for tough times. We are a shaken generation living in a shaken world. We must approach the contemporary scene as the author of the Epistle to the Hebrews viewed his time, namely, as the removing of things that are shaken so that things that cannot be shaken may remain.

Elijah can inspire and challenge us as priests today. The zeal with which he approached his ministry, combined with his ability to recognize the far-reaching implications of what seemed quite innocent and innocuous, helped to expose the dangers of compromise. As priests we have to restore a religious consciousness, creating a sensitivity for God's presence in situations which proclaim his absence. We are called upon to provide support to people who are challenged to move forward yet are tempted to retreat. Like the prophet we have a responsibility to enable people to interpret and evaluate what is uncritically accepted today. For example, something which at first sight seems harmless but which is in fact symptomatic of a whole mentality, namely Sabbath observance. Have we in fact alerted people to what disobedience of the Sabbath implies, recognizing that the Sabbath draws lines of dignity around people ensuring that they are not to be managed or manipulated, that they are related to God? Disrespect for the Sabbath therefore tends to treat people as objects and is in fact a statement about secularization, false gods and idolatry. The message of Elijah is that there is no room for equivocation. The decision of the people to follow God must be clear and uncompromising. That message is necessary today; the choice between God and idols has to be made and ratified continually. Like the prophet we too experience the human frailty of fear, depression, isolation and loneliness. The success which priests savour from time to time cannot hide the fact that much of the priestly ministry is spent in situations of frustration and failure. Neither the prophet nor the priest can abdicate responsibility and opt out of an uncomfortable situation. They must, having received a recommissioning grace from God, set out again on the road that the Lord indicates.

Tenacity in the Midst of Turmoil

Psalm 13 reflects the cry of one who has remained faithful to God despite an experience of God's absence and abandonment similar to that of Elijah. The psalmist comes close to breaking-point, and under the burden of suffering he gives expression to the impatience and anxiety which torment him. Four times in very quick succession he cries out 'how long?' a question which is typical of the psalms of lament. That cry has the effect of taking the present predicament seriously while at the same time it is expressive of the faithful one who feels abandoned by the Lord. It testifies to the fact that a relationship of intimacy and underlying hope still persists. From the impatient anxiety of the opening verse the tone changes in the second verse to one of prayer and supplication. The Lord is invoked in a highly personal way as 'my God'. Though tormented, the psalmist, believing that God is in control and can right the wrong, turns to the Lord who listens to his prayer. The terseness and brevity of the imperatives testify to the sincerity of the prayer:

Look at me, answer me, Lord my God!
Give light to my eyes lest I fall asleep in death.

The lament is intensified by the triumph of the enemy:

lest my enemy say 'I have overcome him';
lest my foes rejoice to see my fall.

The psalmist pleads that God would resume the mutual
relationship which was broken. In the final verse supplication gives way to thanksgiving and praise as the psalmist is
confident that his prayer has been heard. The violent fluctua-
tions at the beginning of the psalm subside as the divine
presence becomes a source of serenity and joy and the
psalmist attributes his happiness to God's *Hesed* , his merciful love:

> As for me, I trust in your merciful love.
> Let my heart rejoice in your saving help.

It is this merciful love which sustains the covenant and
which evokes on our part a hymn of praise:

> Let me sing to the Lord for his goodness to me,
> singing psalms to the name of the Lord, the Most High.

Psalm 13

> How long, O Lord, will you forget me?
> How long will you hide your face?
> How long must I bear grief in my soul,
> this sorrow in my heart day and night?
> How long shall my enemy prevail?
>
> Look at me, answer me, Lord my God!
> give light to my eyes lest I fall asleep in death,
> lest my enemy say: 'I have overcome him';
> lest my foes rejoice to see my fall.
>
> As for me, I trust in your merciful love.
> Let my heart rejoice in your saving help:
> Let me sing to the Lord for his goodness to me
> singing psalms to the name of the Lord, the Most High.

5

Nostalgia or New Creation

There are times in priesthood when everything seems to be going according to a plan. There is a sense of 'being at home' with oneself, a time characterized not merely by absence of tension but even by a feeling of fulfilment and achievement. We feel we have acquired a good understanding of God and are confident about coping with priesthood. Human relationships are not troublesome; faith and prayer give meaning to our ministry. We are undisturbed and uncritical. This experience of order, goodness and reliability suggests a celebration of the status quo.

Then something happens to shatter that convenient and controlled world. We want to hold on to that world where we had the illusion of peace, progress and control; there is a reluctance to let go of it and a corresponding refusal to accept a new situation. This time of dislocation and disorientation is difficult and demanding. We feel threatened as we discover that the pieces which dovetailed so perfectly and with such little effort are now seen to have jagged edges. God, prayer, human relationships, celibacy, priesthood itself all confront us with huge questions. We can identify with the psalmist as he cries out *de profundis*. The difficulty is compounded for us by our inability to articulate the confused and confusing emotions we experience at times like this. The disparity and the distance between appearance and reality quite frequently leaves us speechless and we must suffer in silence. It is a time of testing of nerve and patience. It is psychologically understandable that nostalgia would attempt to neutralize the hurt as people try to cling to old certainties. The tendency is to glamorize the past from a safe distance. By contrast with former times the present appears fruitless and futile. The past is gone, the future is bleak and God appears to be silent. Anger, resentment and fear dominate as we endeavour to come to terms with the new situation.

A counter-movement of re-orientation takes us by surprise, as negative resentful remembering gives way to new hope and fresh expectations. This newness is not simply a re statement of the old, it is genuinely new. The Greek language has two words to denote *new; neos* may be a re-statement or repetition of the old, whereas *kainos* represents what is radically new and unforeseen. In the depths we discover new life and this comes as a surprise to us. Sometimes the present is so painful that it is easy to leave it but more frequently we hesitate to greet the newness of the future because of an insecurity that wants to cling to what we have. Accepting the leanness of the present is a prerequisite for receiving the new joy. That loss-finding, death-life dynamic is central to the three stories in Luke 15, the lost coin, lost sheep and prodigal son. We are astonished that the depths will not hold, that the tomb which had been sealed is empty. We recognize that the lament must not last forever, complaint must not continue, protest and question are not the final word. There is a time for affirmation, a time to end the criticism and celebrate the new reality. This movement from orientation to disorientation and on to a new re-orientation is central to the lament psalms of the Old Testament and is something which may be verified in our own experience.[8]

The Priest in a Time of Orientation

In former times priests in the confessionals raised tired arms in absolution. The sense of sin and of the sacred was unmistakable. People approached their priests with problems and solutions were given clearly and authoritatively. Priesthood had status and appeal and young men were inspired to priestly service. Priesthood was protected; the prayer of priests was regular and regulated; breviary, meditation before and thanksgiving after Mass. Culture and convention separated priests not only from evil but also from much that was good. Friendships with women were frowned upon and we were constantly reminded of the fact that they were souls to be saved, but at a distance. Priesthood then was stable and secure; it was fenced about with fidelity.[9] 'Forever' was firmly implanted in the minds and hearts of the young men who confidently committed themselves.

The Priest in an Exile Situation

Today the old securities and the sociological supports have been removed or reduced. The priest is presented with new demands, fresh expectations, unfamiliar confusions. Priesthood itself as a state means little to people; what matters is this particular priest. We have to earn respect rather than appeal to our profession. We can only offer our priestly witness and many are not convinced of, or are confused about, what this involves. People require that their priests be both one with God and one with them, that they be close, friendly, human, and still be chaste and celibate. These changes are a cause for celebration reminding us that priesthood is not a frozen entity, some great monolithic changeless state. By comparison with an earlier day today's priest ministers in an exile situation.

Exile: The Challenge and the Opportunity

To avail of the opportunities presented by the contemporary scene and to address it with confidence it will be helpful to examine the problems confronting Israel during the period of the exile and the way she coped. Jerusalem was captured in 587 BC, the temple was destroyed and the people, particularly the leading classes, deported to Babylon. They were uprooted, broken and beaten. Yet the marvel is that her history did not end altogether. Israel both survived that calamity, and picking up the pieces, she formed a new community out of the wreckage of the old and resumed her life as God's people. Priesthood today has taken a hammering. Many excellent men have left and we experience the lacuna created by their departure. We torment ourselves in an attempt to find a reason only to discover that there is no satisfactory explanation which could cover all cases. During the Babylonian exile Israel, puzzled by the events, asked questions – is God no longer with us, no longer faithful to his promises? Are the gods of Babylon more powerful? Or is it necessary to reinterpret the present situation and search deeper for God's intentions, for his fidelity and will and for the meaning of what is happening? There was a feeling of being abandoned, as they experienced an eclipse of God. Our questions and experiences are not unlike those of the exiles. The way in which they coped helps to illuminate and interpret our present experience.

The Contribution of Deutero-Isaiah[10]

The exile was the stage on which the theological giant and the greatest mind of all the prophets, Deutero-Isaiah, entered (Isaiah chapters 40-55). There was a mass falling away from the ancestral faith particularly among those who had gone into exile in Babylon at a young age. These were now exposed to the elaborate Babylonian religious pageantry. There was not only a weakening of ties to the faith of their fathers but also a deliberate forgetting of the traditions which had been handed down. One is tempted to ask oneself if that situation does not have parallels with what confronts us today. There are fears, some exaggerated, but many very genuine, that the attempts to receive, transform and pass on many of our sacred traditions have not been successful. In the exilic situation there was, on the one hand, the tragic state of the exiles who were now quickly disappearing in the Babylonian social and religious milieu, but on the other hand there was a small but devoted group of believers whose theological convictions would not permit them to accommodate or compromise. These circumstances presented the

Israelites with opportunities which had not been available in Palestine. It was only after much heart-searching and profound readjustment that their faith survived the crunch.

Prior to the deportation the people had lived secure and self-sufficient. Faith in God had found very distorted expressions. For example the people believed that Jerusalem could not be captured because God was on their side. The repeated warnings of successive prophets had fallen on deaf ears as the people shirked the moral implications of their covenant faith and sheltered in the shadow of the cultic activity of the shrines. Liturgy seemed to have exhausted their religious faith which had very little, if any, relationship with ethical conduct. The unconditional promise to David in 2 Samuel 7 had engendered a false sense of security at the popular level. God and faith were taken for granted and God would be faithful to his promises even if the people were unfaithful to him. Any attempt to inject a note of realism was resented and rejected as Jeremiah discovered when he attempted to shatter the popular misconceptions and the false sense of security engendered by them. Yet it was precisely the catastrophe of the exile which provided the people with the necessary though painful opportunity to purify their faith. One cannot however underestimate the real crisis for faith. The erosion of the supportive quality of certain sociological props had in fact a cathartic value in that religious faith comes to be seen more clearly as a total commitment to God rather than reliance on human structures. Israelite faith not only survived the political disaster of the exile but the people emerged purified and supported by a deeper and broader concept of God after their faith had been significantly purged and depoliticized.

This was not a time to indulge in regret or languish in despair. The people had to avail of the opportunities in which they found themselves now that the familiar supports had vanished. The contribution made in this regard by Deutero-Isaiah, the theologian of the exile was monumental. The way in which he succeeded in helping Israel to break out of a narrow, and at times neurotically, nationalist tradition and examine and incorporate other traditions which deepened rather than negated the ancestral traditions is very interesting and informative and helps to throw light on and provide a ray of hope for our situation today which strongly resembles the theological milieu of the period of exile. Once the 'impossible' had happened and God's unconditional promise to David: 'And your house and your kingdom shall be made sure for ever before me; your throne shall be established forever' (2 Samuel 7.16) was to all appearances broken, there was a deeper search for the Lord's designs and will. Had God's promise failed or had they misinterpreted his work? In the light of their traumatic experience old questions were now asked with a new urgency. The survival of the faith necessitated taking history seriously, particularly their recent history. There would have to be honest heart-searching and serious theological thought. The theology which had prevailed prior to the exile had now taken a severe tumble; it could never re-emerge precisely in that form.

The challenge facing Deutero-Isaiah was two-fold. Firstly, he must interpret and provide a theological explanation for their situation in Babylon. Secondly, and more important, he must provide a ray of hope for the future. The events of the exile were seen as the fulfilment of ancient prophecies, as punishment which was merited by Israel for neglect of the covenant, but a punishment with a purifying intent. This prophet's message is predominantly one of hope and comfort for the exiles, as may be seen from the opening verse:

Comfort, comfort my people,
says your God.
Speak tenderly to Jerusalem,
and cry to her
that her warfare is ended,
that her iniquity is pardoned,
that she has received from the Lord's hand
double for all her sins (Isaiah 40:1-2).

By the time the prophet commenced his prophetic ministry
the political seismographs had already recorded the meteor-
like rise of Cyrus, king of Persia. The development of his
military successes, which was accompanied by a religious
tolerance, awakens in the heart of the exiles an immense
hope. By reinterpreting for them the fast-moving exploits of
Cyrus as the work of the God of Israel, Deutero-Isaiah attempts to dispel the all-pervasive apathy and encourages the
expectation of return to their homeland. The urgency, excite-
ment and fervour arise from his overwhelming conviction
that the Lord is about to create a new future. This message of
hope is determined by the prophet's conception of God. As
creator and Lord of history God cannot be frustrated in his
designs, not even by the chaos of the Babylonian exile. His
choice of Cyrus as the human instrument serves to underpin
his control of history.

A New Exodus

The return from Babylon is depicted in terms of a new
exodus. Belief in salvation was at the very core of Israelite
faith. Their understanding of salvation only gradually, and
at times painfully, outgrew a narrow nationalism. Old Testament faith has two focal points, the creation of the world
which involves all mankind, and the exodus which involves
the chosen people. Between these points there was a tension
and movements of attraction and repulsion. Deutero-Isaiah
realized he must, with the aid of these doctrines, reinterpret
the events of the exile, placing them in the broader context of
the Lord's over-all plan. The exiles need to be reassured that
God is still in control, despite the appearances, and is supe-
rior to the Babylonian gods. The prophet is therefore faced
with explaining the apparent lack of divine activity and so
must counter the complaints of those who lack faith and the
apostasy of those who are drawn to worship other gods. This
determines that the prophet looks both to the past and to the
future. Like his predecessors he categorically lays the blame
squarely on the shoulders of the people. But in doing so he

also takes care to broaden and magnify their concept of God realizing that only such a God will be capable of restoring the people. This the prophet achieves by emphasizing God as creator, as controller of history and redeemer:

> Thus says the Lord, your redeemer,
> who formed you from the womb!
> 'I am the Lord, who made all things,
> who stretched out the heavens alone,
> who spread out the earth who
> was with me?' (Isaiah 44:24).

At this time the Zion tradition, based as we have seen on the unconditional promise to David in 2 Samuel 7, was in ruins, while the Mosaic tradition still depended on the concept of a national God whose position was reflected in the political situation of the nation. To break out of this theological straight-jacket and incorporate a universalism which would enable the exiles to view the events in a different light Deutero-Isaiah goes back beyond the exodus to seek a statement of the cosmic supremacy of the Lord. It is not sufficient for the exiles to hear that God was creator at the beginning of time. His activity must be a present one if it is to answer their questions. This the prophet illustrates by depicting the return in terms reminiscent of both creation and exodus, so that what God is doing in restoring the people to their homeland is none other than a new act of creation; as such his salvific activity is a continuation of his creative concern. This enables the prophet to move very quickly from creation to the Lord's control of history where he introduces Cyrus as God's agent in liberating the people from Babylonian captivity. That he can choose a pagan as his instrument in the redemption of his chosen people serves to broaden the historical horizon and underpins the cosmic supremacy of the Lord. The Israelites therefore, must look beyond their own circumscribed community to the whole civilized world if they are to behold the glory and majesty of God's purpose in history.

Nostalgia

One of the great themes in Israelite faith, the central one, was the exodus. This was the time of Israel's creation by the Lord:

> But now thus says the Lord,
> he who created you, O Jacob,
> he who formed you, O Israel,
> Fear not, for I have redeemed you,
> I have called you by name, you are mine (Isaiah 43:1).

This prophet is in keeping with the general Old Testament mentality of recalling the great works of God in the past as a motive for faith in the future. The events of former times are a type of the future and people lived between a memory and an expectation, an exodus in the past and one in the future. The fundamental resistance which Deutero-Isaiah encountered was resistance to hope. Just as the Israelites had complained and murmured against God and against Moses at the time of the exodus, so now those in exile, not unlike ourselves, grow tired and protest. They are afraid and enslaved by nostalgia; they are obstinate and feel let down and abandoned by God. The prophet of the exile takes this broken, resigned and dispirited people and gives them hope:

> Can a woman forget her sucking child,
> that she should have no compassion
> on the son of her womb?
> Even these may forget,
> yet, I will not forget you.
> Behold, I have graven you on the
> psalms of my hands (Isaiah 49:15-16).

His entire message is one of hope and he insists that people must remain open to this hope. Two attitudes militate against hope. Firstly, taking refuge nostalgically in the past, thus depriving the future of its meaning. It is akin to a driver who is so preoccupied with the rear-view mirror as to lose sight of the road ahead. The second attitude which militates against hope is to deny the newness of the future.[11] This leads to a sort of cynical scepticism – not uncommon today among priests – the attitude of the world-weary Ecclesiastes of the Old Testament, summed up in his refrain 'there is nothing new under the sun' (Ecclesiastes 1:9). Deutero-Isaiah's message is 'do not be preoccupied with the past, God is active also in the present and is not exhausted by former wonders like the exodus'.

New Creation

The new event cannot be fully encapsulated in the former ones:

Remember not the former things,
nor consider the things of old.
Behold, I am doing a new thing (Isaiah 43:18-19).

The 'former things' in this context refer to the events of the exodus, while the 'new thing' refers to the actions which God is about to accomplish in delivering his people from exile. A glorification of the past would blind them to the actions of God in the present. There is a lesson there for all of us. The people are therefore told not to become preoccupied with the exodus tradition, with the past of their nation. While the new deliverance is depicted against the backdrop of the former yet the prophet recognizes that the new cannot possibly be understood, interpreted or encapsulated solely in terms of the former event. To express this tension Deutero-Isaiah contrasts the events; the exodus from Egypt was in flight, the return from Babylonian captivity will be a triumphant march:

For you shall not go out in haste,
and you shall not go in flight,
for the Lord will go before you,
and the God of Israel will be your
rear guard (Isaiah 52:12).

The new event is not just a repetition of the original in cyclic fashion. It is radically new, unprecedented and unique. The Lord is a living God whose power controls the present; he is not exhausted by the glories of the past:

> The Lord is an everlasting God,
> the creator of the ends of the earth,
> He does not faint or grow weary,
> His understanding is unsearchable.
> He gives power to the faint,
> and to him who has no might
> he increases strength.
> Even youths shall faint and be weary
> and young men shall fall exhausted;
> but they who wait for the Lord shall
> renew their strength,
> they shall mount up with wings like eagles,
> they shall run and not be weary,
> they shall walk and not faint (Isaiah 40:28-31).

The exiles had a rather circumscribed view of God whom they had cut down to size in their covenant faith and liturgical celebrations. They had created a god in their own image, a comfortable, predictable one whom they could manipulate at will. Deutero-Isaiah succeeds in broadening their concept of God so that they can recognize what he is saying to them through the turbulent events of Babylonian exile.

In our own situation today the sociological supports are quickly disappearing. It is a time for genuine faith when people will be Christian by conviction rather than by convention, by their own act of faith attained in a difficult struggle and perpetually achieved anew. The supports which had been available for faith and priesthood in the past are not now so obvious and, in many areas, are in fact working in diametrical opposition. Many priests find this not just challenging but quite confusing. We find no stability in a society which is in constant flux where the accepted values of the past are being challenged, where moral codes are in the melting-pot, and where everything is fluctuating. The Church is caught up in this storm of change like a little boat in strange new waters. Some rush to the left, others to the right, some are shining up the masts to peer ahead, others are endeavouring to drop anchor at the stern. This makes the work of the priest more difficult and demanding.

Yet, there is a great richness and vitality emerging in the Church. The interest in and attendance at adult religious education courses testifies to groups who recognize the importance and relevance of their faith in today's world. Along with Eucharistic ministers, lay readers, Catholic marriage advisory council, prayer groups and parish councils these people are all anxious to provide a ministry of service within the Church. Prior to the development of a theology of ministry people had been providing dedicated service in groups like St Vincent de Paul, Legion of Mary, Apostolic Workers, Pioneer Total Abstinence Association. Whether the latter are falling on lean times due to lack of support and encouragement from priests is difficult to say. All of this makes fresh demands on the priest, so priests must avail of the opportunity to harness this tremendous source of goodwill for Christ and the Church. In the midst of all of this there are times when we bemoan the straightforward, predictable, security of a bygone age. Yet through these events God is speaking to us and we need to be alert to the situation if we are to support the people involved in these ventures, deepen their faith and enable them to make their contribution in building up the Kingdom of God.

By a careful evaluation of today's exile situation the Church will be enabled to determine its approach for the future. Differences between Church and world are emerging more sharply with the consequent clarification of the ecclesial agenda. As the Church becomes free of entanglements, obligations, involvements and claims which had accumulated around her historically the world is provided with a fresh access to this Church. In this situation men and women will be Christians not by custom and tradition but only by an act of deep faith. As the Church weighs anchor and spreads her sails to the breeze we find ourselves living in, listening and responding to an exilic situation which has certain affinities with the situation confronting the Babylonian exiles and for which Deutero-Isaiah undertook a courageous and critical re-examination.

Past, Present, and Future

Psalm 42-43

The psalms fully expose the problem of depression and despair. The faith to which they witness does not skate on the surface of life, rather it plumbs the depths and soars to the heights of human experience. Together these psalms form one poem of three strophes marked by an identical refrain:

> Why are you cast down, my soul,
> why groan within me?
> Hope in God; I will praise him still,
> my saviour and my God

which has the effect of changing the tone and dividing the poem into past, present and future. The psalmist, a refugee forced to dwell far from his native land, and possibly one of the Babylonian exiles, expresses in deeply moving words the sufferings he had to endure as he sojourns far away from Jerusalem and its temple. Pining away for those privileged moments which he spent in intimate communion with God in the temple he now lives in a state of deprivation where he is confronted by a pagan environment where God and religious values are mocked:

> as I hear it said all the day long:
> 'where is your God?'

In a deeply moving lamentation the psalmist pours out his soul.

In the first strophe water is seen as a symbol of life, in the second it becomes a symbol of death and destruction. In a mountainous region the author catches a glimpse of a parched deer frantically searching for water. This expresses the anxious state of mind of the psalmist in his longing for God. For the animal water is life-sustaining in an arid landscape. The search for God acquires something of this fundamental instinct of conservation for the poet:

My soul is thirsting for God,
the God of my life;

He recalls a past already long gone. In a moving dialogue with his own soul the psalmist, realizing that a whining self-pity will achieve nothing, chides his emotional nature for its despondency and complaint:

Why are you cast down, my soul,
why groan within me?

The way out of darkness is expressed in the following line:

Hope in God; I will praise him still,
my saviour, and my God.

This involves bearing the tension of his life in the strength of faith. So while nostalgia, discouragement and depression dominate, yet at a more profound level faith and hope begin to emerge.

In the second strophe the image changes and in the thunder of the waves cascading down the mountain the psalmist contemplates the tension and turmoil of his own soul in his adversity. This strophe is dominated by the present lean experience of the psalmist as he is exposed to the rebukes of his enemies:

with cries that pierce me to the heart,
my enemies revile me,
saying to me all the day long:
'Where is your God?'

At the very centre of this strophe however a strong note of hope resounds:

> By day the Lord will send
> His loving kindness;
> by night I will sing to him,
> praise the God of my life.

We can detect here a state of emotional change, common in many of the psalms of supplication, as the God of the glorious past becomes the God of future fulfilment, recalling the words of Deutero-Isaiah:

> Remember not the former things,
> nor consider the things of old.
> Behold, I am doing a new thing;
> now it springs forth, do you not
> perceive it? (Isaiah 43:18-19).

In the third strophe the poet directs his thoughts to the prospect of hope in and help from God as he tenaciously clings to his faith in the Lord. This enables him to cope with the rebukes of his adversaries. Here past and future join hands in a cry of triumph as what had once been a melancholy recollection becomes a symbol of hope.

In our experience as priests we are acutely aware of the apparent absence of God. Frequently this experience has a cathartic result in helping to correct false ideas of a God who is available and manipulable. Our desire for God however has a sustaining power enabling us to confront fear and frustration. There will always be something of the presence/ absence tension in our relationship with God as he takes us by surprise and breaks out of the narrow confines to which we subject him. This loss/finding, death/life dynamic is central to a God who continues to take us by surprise. He cannot remain the object of our nostalgia for the past; we have an appointment with him in the future towards which he beckons us in faith.

Psalm 42

Like the deer that yearns
for running streams,
so my soul is yearning
for you, my God.

My soul is thirsting for God
the God of my life;
when can I enter and see
the face of God?

My tears have become my bread,
by night, by day,
as I hear it said all the day long:
'Where is your God?'

These things will I remember
as I pour out my soul:
how I would lead the rejoicing crowd
into the house of God,
amid cries of gladness and thanksgiving,
the throng wild with joy.

Why are you cast down, my soul,
why groan within me?
Hope in God; I will praise him still,
my saviour and my God.

My soul is cast down within me
as I think of you,
from the country of Jordan and Mount Hermon,
from the Hill of Mizar.

Deep is calling on deep,
in the roar of waters:
your torrents and all your waves
swept over me.

By day the Lord will send
his loving kindness;

by night I will sing to him,
praise the God of my life.

I will say to God, my rock:
'Why have you forgotten me?
Why do I go mourning
oppressed by the foe?'

With cries that pierce me to the heart,
my enemies revile me,
saying to me all the day long:
'Where is your God?'

Why are you cast down, my soul,
why groan within me?
Hope in God; I will praise him still,
my saviour and my God.

Psalm 43

Defend me, O God, and plead my cause
against a godless nation.
From deceitful and cunning men
rescue me, O God.

Since you, O God, are my stronghold,
why have you rejected me?
Why do I go mourning
oppressed by the foe?

O send forth your light and your truth;
let these be my guide.
Let them bring me to your holy mountain
to the place where you dwell.

And I will come to the altar of God,
the God of my joy,
My redeemer, I will thank you on the harp,
O God, my God.

Why are you cast down, my soul,

why groan within me?
Hope in God; I will praise him still,
my saviour and my God.

6

Mary: Creative Courage

A Path-Finder for the Priest

We live at a time when one age is dying and a new age is not yet born. We witness around us radical changes in religion, in marriage styles and family structures, in sexual morality, in technology and indeed in almost every area of modern life. Many would admit to being quite perplexed about all of this. Priesthood is inevitably affected as we endeavour to respond to these changes in a positive manner and confront them with the word of God of which we are ministers. This leaves priests quite confused and perplexed. This is not the priesthood to which I committed myself ten, twenty, forty years ago. To live with sensitivity in this age of limbo requires great courage. We are faced with a choice which amounts to either a negative or a positive reaction. As we experience a shaking of the foundations there is the temptation, psychologically understandable, to recoil panic-stricken. Frightened by the loss of our mooring places in the safe havens, we yield to a form of mental and pastoral paralysis as apathy takes over. Should this be our reaction then we will have abdicated our responsibility for the formation of the future. On the contrary if we choose to react and respond positively to the changed and changing circumstances then courage will be necessary to keep us sensitive and aware of our responsibilities. If we choose this course, and as priests we are obliged to, we need a path-finder and who can serve that role better than Mary the mother of God?[12]

When summoned to do something new Mary declared herself available. The path to a hope-filled future was trodden by her. At the annunciation St Luke presents her as being 'greatly troubled' (Luke 1:29) by the angel's greeting which recognized a special relationship between herself and God, 'Hail full of grace, the Lord is with you' (Luke 1:28). We may legitimately extend that perplexity at the time of Mary's call. Perplexity, confusion and questioning, as well as uncertainty would characterize Mary's life from that time on. She did not receive any specific or detailed explanation of God's message. She was being asked to sign a blank cheque. Mary was not a woman to whom the future was foreseeable, she possessed no programme in the palm of her hand.

We can identify with her on that score. When we walked wide-eyed out of the Chapel on ordination day we did not possess any specific God-given scenario for our ministry. We did not know in detail what God's call involved; we only knew, like Mary, that it was he who was calling. As with Mary, God was only informing us of the first step. As the years moved on the story of our call would be written and the details would be inserted. As with Mary there would be confusion and questions, wonder and uncertainty, changes and surprises, thorns and crosses. God's call whether then or now reveals very little, the skeleton call, the bare bones. This call requires unbelievable faith on the part of the addressee, it requires the placing of our hand in the hand of God. He promises that he will be present and will remain faithful though we may be absent and unfaithful. God provides us only with sufficient detail to evoke our declaration of availability. Mary responded: 'Behold, I am the handmaid of the Lord: let it be to me according to your word' (Luke 1:38). Mary's greatness may be located in her faith that God could and would fulfil his promise through her. With her response she becomes the first Christian disciple and the annunciation may be seen as her calling to discipleship. Her life marks her as a model for the followers of Jesus. In the infancy story Luke writes with hindsight and foreshadows the way in which he will present her in the Gospel proper where she is seen as one who hears the word of God and acts upon it. She lives what the Gospel proclaims. Doing the will of God said St Augustine is of greater value even than having borne Jesus.

Mary: Attentive to God at the Annunciation

Those who may have grown lukewarm in devotion to Mary should pay more attention to the evidence provided by Luke and John. In the annunciation scene she is depicted as being in continuity with the line of Old Testament prophets, receiving the word of God in a crisis situation for the people; in Mary's case the word is the word made flesh, Jesus Christ. The great classical prophets recognized their limitations, Jeremiah claiming he was too young and a poor speaker (1:6), Isaiah giving the excuse that he was unworthy, 'a man of unclean lips' (6:5). Their inadequacy was underlined in order to highlight God's contribution. This sets the theme of God's call and his powerful presence with the human agent in bold relief. Like the prophets Mary acknowledges the human difficulties: 'How can this be since I have no husband' (Luke 1:34). As priests we are very conscious of the difficulties surrounding us and have probably counter-acted by making excuses for not becoming involved and carrying out the full implications of God's word. We resemble the Israelites when they were close to the land of Canaan in the Book of Numbers chapters thirteen and fourteen. God's word assures them that the country was theirs and invites them to enter and take possession of it. However the reality did not seem to correspond to the declaration. The question is what will be used as a basis for their decision, will it be the divine promise, the word of God, or will it be the human evaluation? On that occasion the people became demoralized at the pessimistic reports of the scouts who had been sent ahead to spy out the land. A similar temptation confronts the priest. If instead of trusting completely the word of God we look for human assurance then our steps will become unsteady, our approach and outlook will be timid and troubled. The ideal which we glimpse will appear illusory and incapable of being lived. We will give way to confusion and will yield to obstacles. Our lack of faith will militate against the full realization of God's promise and as a result we become protectors of self rather than preachers of God. No longer confident that God can and will accomplish his plan through us, we become deaf to his grace and opt for mediocrity.

The objections of Isaiah and Jeremiah were not entertained by God. He reassures them that he will be with his chosen instrument. Mary is reminded that the human difficulties will be overcome: 'The Holy Spirit will come upon you, and the power of the Most High will overshadow you; therefore the child to be born will be called holy, the Son of God' (Luke 1:35). In our ministry we are familiar with moments of reassurance which probably do not come as frequently as we would wish, but which, when they come, are times when God's powerful presence is very real, when we know that He is unmistakably with us and we are given unambiguous signs. The sign which Mary was given was the sign of Elizabeth's pregnancy which defied the barrenness of years and the ordinary course of human events. In presenting the annunciation to Mary in terms of the call which the prophets of the Old Testament received, the third evangelist indicates that she is in continuity with God's saving wisdom of former times and, like the prophets, her role is one of active and conscious co-operation with God.

The Priest and The Word of God

Priests have a particular responsibility for the word of God, for listening to, reflecting on, preaching and sharing that word with others. The words of instruction in the rite of ordination are very forceful and informative: 'They (priests) are called to share in the priesthood of the Bishops and to be moulded into the likeness of Christ, the supreme and eternal High Priest. By consecration they will be made true priests of the New Testament, *to preach the Gospel,* sustain God's people and celebrate the liturgy above all the Lord's sacrifice. . . . My sons you are now about to be advanced to the order of the presbyterate. You must apply your energies to the duty of teaching in the name of Christ, the chief teacher, *share with all mankind the word of God* you have received with joy. *Meditate on the law of Christ,* believe what you read, teach what you believe and put into practice what you teach. *Let the doctrine you teach be true nourishment for the people of God.* Let the example of your lives attract the followers of Christ, so that by *word* and *action* you may build up the house which is God's Church '

Honesty determines we admit that we frequently recoil from the responsibilities demanded by God's word. At times we listen to and reflect upon it but for lack of courage and conviction and a fear of rejection we fail to preach, teach and share that word with boldness. On other occasions we manufacture situations in which we do not and cannot listen to and reflect on God's word. Mary was presented by Luke as one who made space in her life so that the word of God could enter. She created a zone of silence which enabled her to say 'yes' to God. His word needs space, time, and silence. Preaching to a highly-educated, media-conditioned, people determines that our approach be professional and that we avail of the various skills of communication, but in our anxiety to make the message relevant, attractive and appealing there is the real danger of compromising the content.

'Let it be to me according to your word' (Luke 1:38), is not a once-for-all affirmation. It grows more demanding with the years, when God's word is spoken in very human even harsh situations. Men ordained twenty years or more would have been very conscious of joining a winning team, but today the rising tides of secularism, cynicism and doubt have dispelled that illusion. In Mary we have a blueprint for hearing the word of God and reflecting on it. Mary at the annunciation 'considered in her mind what sort of greeting this might be' (Luke 1:29) and at the birth of Jesus 'Mary kept all these things, pondering them in her heart' (Luke 2:19).

Accepting God's word, Mary brings to the plan of salvation her faith that the Lord would accomplish something great in her. This faith stands in stark contrast to the doubt of Zechariah who disbelieved the Lord's word.

As priests we may be too close to stand back and analyze our own vocations. In reading the annunciation to Mary we are enabled to recognize different elements and influences at work within our own situation. Priesthood today is being lived out at a rather critical time for religious faith and a time when traditional values are being quickly eroded and presented as old-fashioned and out-moded by the false prophets. Having received God's word Mary quickly realizes the implication of sharing it with others and putting it into practice. The first recorded event after the annunciation is the visitation: 'Mary arose and went with haste into the hill country, to a city of Judah and she entered the house of Zechariah and greeted Elizabeth' (Luke 1:39). That combination of prayer and action, prayer inspiring the action, so obvious in Mary's life is something we need to foster in our own lives and to teach to others. That two-fold emphasis has continued to be the approach of the Legion of Mary. Into the infancy story Luke reads back Mary's reactions from the rest of the Gospel. In the Gospel proper Jesus proclaims: 'my mother and my brethren are those who hear the word of God and do it' (Luke 8:21). To the woman in the crowd who cries aloud: 'Blessed is the womb that bore you, and the breasts that you sucked' (Luke 11:27), Jesus responds: 'Blessed rather are those who hear the word of God and keep it' (Luke 11:28). Any dichotomy between word and action leads to self-deception: 'Be doers of the word and not hearers only, deceiving yourselves' (Epistle of James 1:22).

Cana: Mary's Concern for Others

If the annunciation scene revealed Mary as alert to the divine dimension of life, the episode at the wedding of Cana in John 2:1-11 underlines her attentiveness to the human dimension. Here she joins in the festivities but is capable of detachment which determines that she is not enslaved by them. A discreet attention to what is taking place keeps her alert to something which has escaped the attention of others; the wine had run short. She has an overview of the situation which ensures that everything is seen in perspective and so given its appropriate value. She is sensitive to the situation, recognizes the distress, and can empathize with embarrassed hosts and. guests. Her gift of synthesis, typically feminine, is something we need today. Without it the Church runs the risk of becoming a society of experts preoccupied with plugging our own programme, but too efficient to provide a service. Mary's approach at Cana must cause us to ask whether we have become so programmed and preoccupied with our personal responsibilities and trivialities that we lose sight of anything which falls outside the area of competence which we like to champion. She does not assume the role of problem-solver directly. Her response takes place on a double plane, indicative and imperative. She entrusts the situation to Jesus in the indicative mood: 'they have no wine' (John 2:3), and to the servants in the imperative: 'do whatever he tells you' (John 2:5).

In doing so Mary avoids two mistaken tendencies which are very real temptations facing the priest today.[13] Firstly, she avoids the tendency to moralize and deplore failure in difficult circumstances. Religion always runs the risk of moralizing in order to make us better people, but that attempt is futile if it fails to recognize the primitive helplessness of others and resorts to nailing men and women to their sinful past, their negative experiences and their guilt. The other tendency which Mary avoids is the temptation to show a benign tolerance to everything, an indifference that is aloof and, by implication, declares that there is no hierarchy of values. Today this is a real temptation for the priest who accepts people *as* they are but is prepared to leave them *where* they are.

In our ministry we need Mary's contemplative approach if we are to examine our celebrations and recognize what is lacking, the things which deprive others and ourselves of peace and joy. Contemplation saves us from arrogance in our relationship with God and also from manipulation of others. The decline in vocations causes many priests to feel plagued with pressures, some of which are inevitable, many are accidental, while others are self-induced, as priests live in permanent over-drive. In that situation we sense that there is something lacking in our ministry but we are frequently so preoccupied that we find it difficult to be precise about what is missing. We need Mary to help us in making that discovery. There is confidence, conviction and courage in Mary's approach, expressed in her advice to the servants 'do whatever he tells you'. She takes this step in faith and her words win an abundance for those in need. Faith in the power of Christ has dictated her approach. As priests we need to learn the way of contemplation and share it with others so that they will recognize the primacy of contemplation as preceding any worthwhile pastoral activity.

Hope Transforms History

In the Magnificat we catch a glimpse of Mary's vision of a new world where the proud will be humbled and the lowly exalted; where the rich will be sent empty away and the hungry filled with good things. The stark contrasts have something of the radical ring of the beatitudes about them:

> Blessed are the meek, for they shall
> inherit the earth (Matthew 5:5).

> Blessed are those who hunger and
> thirst for righteousness, for they shall
> be satisfied (Matthew 5:6).

> Blessed are the poor in spirit,
> for theirs is the kingdom of heaven (Matthew 5:3).

Priests have visions of the work they would like to do and the society they would wish to create. The value of Mary's vision lies in the fact that it is a Christian vision. There she displays creative courage and discovers new forms and patterns on which a new society may be structured. In her hymn of praise, which reverberates with echoes of the psalms, of Hannah's praise of God (1 Samuel 2:1-10) and other mosaics of the Old Testament, Mary praises the Lord of the covenant for his loving mercy and fidelity. Focusing on the power and presence of God she gives birth to a new reality which gives priority to the poor, the dispossessed, the marginalized and the victims of the present order who testify to God's judgment on our society. In this respect Mary threatens the social order in a creative constructive manner and is a symbol of hope. The Magnificat contains three revolutions, firstly a moral one:

> He puts forth his arm in strength
> and scatters the proud-hearted (Luke 1:51),

secondly a social one:

> He casts the mighty from their thrones
> and raises the lowly (Luke 1:52),

and finally an economic revolution:

> He fills the starving with good things,
> sends the rich away empty (Luke 1:53).

In the Magnificat then Mary approaches history from the standpoint of hope. Despite suffering and injustice she contemplates the coming of God who 'makes all things new' (Revelation 21:5) and transforms human existence. The hymn begins with the personal experience 'My soul glorifies the Lord' and then immediately zones in on what God has done. We witness there the perfect balance between the personal experience and the contemplation of God, which should enable us to critically evaluate some modern approaches to spirituality.

Magnificat (Luke 1:46-55)

My soul glorifies the Lord,
my spirit rejoices in God, my Saviour.
He looks on his servant in her lowliness;
henceforth all ages will call me blessed.

The Almighty works marvels for me.
Holy his name!
His mercy is from age to age,
on those who fear him.

He puts forth his arm in strength
and scatters the proud-hearted.
He casts the mighty from their thrones
and raises the lowly.

He fills the starving with good things,
sends the rich away empty.

He protects Israel, his servant,
remembering his mercy,
the mercy promised to our fathers,
to Abraham and his sons for ever.

7

Celibacy and Sexuality

In view of the many negative things which have been written about it in recent years it is hardly surprising that one who endeavours to portray celibacy in a positive way would be classified as self-righteous, conservative, uninformed, unwilling to change, immature, too idealistic, well-intentioned but naive. In many ways our approach to celibacy will be determined by whether we live by fear or by hope, whether we are pessimists or optimists. The most frequently repeated command in the Bible is 'fear not'. The pessimist is powerless and alone against what may be considered insurmountable difficulties; the optimist does not underestimate the difficulties but recognizes that we do not stand alone. 'I am with you' is a frequent follow on to the imperative 'fear not'. Is it not the case that pessimists are frequently credited with having a better grasp of reality than optimists, being more intelligent and insightful? Pessimists are frequently infectious and grant a grudging condescending toleration to those who do not share their perspective. Faith and hope are indispensable elements in any meaningful discussion of Christian celibacy and it is against that background that I propose to deal with the subject.

Someone said that celibacy is a bit like going on a bread and water diet. When one goes on such a diet there must be more to it than abstaining. A person who eats when hungry needs no further reason for that action. But the one who fasts although hungry does require a reason beyond the fasting itself. Similarly with celibacy, there must be more than a state of being unmarried, of abstaining from sexual relationships. Celibacy does not have a built-in meaning like eating or marriage. As celibates we tend to discuss celibacy itself. It is odd how we always speak of celibacy in general. Celibacy does not exist in the abstract. Only celibates exist, so to take refuge in generalities about such a subject is misguided, dangerous and self-defeating. It is important that we re-evaluate ourselves and ask not about celibacy itself, but how things are going with *my celibacy*. New questions may have arisen for me since I last gave serious consideration to my living out of celibacy. Does it witness to Christ or to my own egoism? Merely human renunciation is not necessarily virtue. It has to be chosen for God's sake. It leads to a way of being, not of functioning, so we do not take a vow of celibacy in order that we might work more effectively and efficiently, but we do make such a vow in order that we might live more fully a life totally dependant on faith in God.

Celibacy is a choice of one value among many. It is very significant that the first statement made about man in the Bible expresses God's assessment: 'it is not good that the man should be alone' (Genesis 2:18). The Yahwist, who has always been credited with a keen insight into human psychology, highlights the social nature of man. Sexuality is a gift so that we might live in fellowship; it is a gift of God expressing the fact that we are relational beings. In this context it is important to stress that many of the problems which confront us in celibate life are not problems which face us because we are celibate but simply because we are human. There has been such a heavy rather than a healthy concentration on what the celibate sacrifices that it has been very difficult to see any real value it may offer the Church in the context of proclaiming the Gospel and announcing the kingdom of God. As long as it is seen as the avoiding of relationships it will be viewed as narrow, negative, and neurotic. If the concentration is on another world while neglecting the reality of the kingdom as it is present here and now, though only partially, then celibacy will be unreal and unconvincing. What do we renounce as celibates? We do not renounce our sexuality, but we renounce means of expression of this which are out of keeping with the orientation we have chosen. Strength, sensitivity, gentleness and warmth are particular channels by which God's love becomes incarnate and is mediated to others, provided that these are unambiguous, clear and restricted as such. Tenderness is love that is respectful, practical, joyful, not mean, not grasping, not pretentious or possessive, but strong in its own weakness. On another level we renounce the ultimate and faithful companionship of a beloved, that intimate complementarity of man and woman which brings joy and security, for example the sharing of secrets, of intimate presence and promises, consolations and mutual responsibilities.

Integration of Sexuality

Unfortunately quite frequently what is projected of the prude is mistakenly seen as appropriate to the celibate. Integration of sexuality marks the difference between them although they both refrain from a particular form of expression, namely, erotic love. The prude is preoccupied with sex, experiences guilt and repulsion when dealing with the prostitute and sex addict. Because the prude cannot cope with such people or situations, he can only resort to criticism and condemnation, the prude cannot provide these men and women with new life. By contrast the celibate can be at ease with such people. He can make contact with the experience of Christ who loved Mary Magdelene without communicating with her in erotic terms or communing with her on a sexual level. Like Jesus in that situation with Mary Magdelene the celibate too has the power to redeem and renew precisely because he can be at home with such people without relating at a sensuous level.

Celibate Relationships

As celibates we strive after friendship but are also prepared to live without its constant presence. Personal growth and self-esteem require human relationships. But we know from experience that celibate friendships are not easily acquired. They have to be geared in a celibate direction. As celibates we are required to take risks but this also implies being realistic about where a relationship may be going. A celibate relationship involves the non-exclusive, unpossessive, total acceptance of another. It demands a degree of emotional maturity which is not guaranteed by age. Genuine friendships can make us better priests by increasing our capacity for love of God and of others. But where friendship is merely a psychological compensation for the emotional and physical satisfaction which we renounce in the vow then maturity becomes stunted and an obstacle to celibacy must be recognized. If friendship becomes not merely a substitute but in fact provides the emotional and physical satisfaction which we have renounced then, try as we may to rationalize, we cannot justify it. As celibates it is important to recognize when we are two-timing. The celibate must ask the question, 'am I free in my relationships', free to enter into, empathize with, and support others or is there a relationship in my life which deprives me of that freedom and which is absorbing more and more of my time and attention? What about prayer, house and school visitation or any other area of priesthood? Are these suffering because I am absorbed by someone else and invariably gravitate towards that person? On the other hand I must ask myself do I leave others free? Or do I pressurize and manipulate them? Do I create a dependency which I can utilize and enjoy? Do I demand frequent contact and recognition and sulk if these are not forthcoming? Being celibate means that one owns no one and is owned by no one. We are close to and involved with others but are not anybody's property or exclusive preserve.

While each celibate relationship is unique, it can never be exclusive in the sense that it bars a similar sharing of love with others; it cannot afford to be limiting or narrowing. To prevent our love from becoming restrictive or confining, as celibates we cannot offer ourselves or express our love in a way that automatically limits the offer to one person alone. The gift of oneself must be open to everyone. The attitude therefore should be one of sharing in such a way that it can become a multiple sharing. There should be no competition among those with whom one might share. No one person becomes the centre of our life to the extent that everyone else must be secondary. While we might think more of one person than anyone else, this particularity in itself does not place a limit on what we share with others. We must do justice to the fact that every relationship is unique so I do not envisage that we share equally with everyone. Because each person is unique, and because one person will be more compatible and receptive than another, inequality in our celibate relationships is unavoidable. However, respect for the uniqueness of each relationship should prevent us from comparing and contrasting relationships. True celibate love removes the basis for jealousy, since the love is diffusive. By its nature it wants to share with as many as possible so it never excludes the possibility of any person whatever coming into the relationship and sharing it. A useful practical guide would be to hold oneself open to the possibility of sharing with others in the same manner as one shares with this person.

Exclusiveness is one of the special attractions of sexual love in marriage, much of its meaning is lost if it is not exclusive. Universality is one of the characteristics of celibate love; the celibate makes every effort to remain free of involvements and expressions of love that tend towards or foster exclusiveness. The celibate therefore does not use secrets, self-revelations or selective gifts to build an exclusive love, directed to one person but withheld from others. If feelings of jealousy and resentment are experienced when others get close to one's friend this may well be a sign that the person is seen as someone to possess rather than to love. The celibate must remain free and must maintain the freedom of the other. In mature celibate love there is no demand for any kind of response. The other is not put under obligation or the promise of fidelity. True celibate love will never cause a person to choose between me and another. All-embracing, it precludes this choice between people. There is a strong human tendency to want certain kinds of response. Like everyone else the celibate likes to be affirmed – and by the right people. However, the true celibate never demands these responses. Nor is he disposed to accept an expression of love that would limit that person's love for others. The joy is located in receiving love that bears the impulse of freedom, the freedom to love others in the same way. Protecting one's relationships by the security that is normally associated with possessiveness or a promise of fidelity is a psychologically understandable temptation. This however limits the freedom of sharing and begins to limit the diffusive character of celibate love. To give oneself to others without an assurance of some return determines that the celibate be a source of goodness for these rather than a demand on them; this illustrates the nature of celibate love where no one is bound to another except through a very free response and a free gift of self. The celibate does not need the assurance of a return of his love because it is rooted in the goodness of giving not in the psychological need of receiving in order to grow.

It may be helpful to re-state the obvious. There are warning signals that our love may be moving away from celibacy. The first and obvious one, when the expression of one's love becomes physical. Secondly, when one feels jealous or resents others getting close to one's friend. Thirdly, when one considers the other person as ours or feels bound by a sense of duty or loyalty towards them. Fourthly, when one expects or demands certain kinds of response. Fifthly, when one's ability to reason with clarity becomes diminished leading to a lack of availability for and commitment to one's duty especially pastoral visitation, because of one's emotional involvement with another. Finally, when one's involvement with another causes us to lose our appetite for prayer.[14]

Celibacy and Faith

Celibacy may be chosen for many reasons. Too often I feel we attempt to understand it in cultural and psychological terms. It only makes sense, however, in relation to one's faith in and response to Jesus Christ. We are called to discipleship and celibacy is a positive choice of the single life for the sake of Christ in response to the call of God. However one's celibacy does not prove God's transcendence rather one's whole way of life expresses faith in it. As a counter-sign in a society, celibacy invites that society to an awareness of the fact that love and not pleasure is the goal of human sexuality; that God and not comfort is the goal of man. It insists that love centres around the heart, not around the sexual organs. In 1914 Teilhard de Chardin claimed that human development would cease, become fixated and even regress if man's sexuality were to be directed by chemical and mechanical means. Christian celibacy has something very important to contribute to our understanding of mankind. We sometimes speak as if all the alternatives which life offers can be really lived. But when all is said and done we cannot first tentatively explore each different opportunity life offers and then go back to start living the one that suits us best. There is much in human life we can only experience by sacrificing. We can serenely trust the Gospel only if we know in our bones that we must make a choice. The eternal business of comparing advantages between marriage and celibacy is futile and destined to failure.

Celibacy and Eucharist

Is the celibacy which I have chosen part of my act of faith? To attempt to answer that question I consider it important to place celibacy in the context of the Eucharist. The Eucharist anticipates the final victory; there Jesus makes my future present to me in himself. It is a pledge of future resurrection and a ground of hope. Like the Eucharist the life of the celibate must witness to Jesus as Lord of history. The life of the celibate is a life of radical and total hope in Jesus.

Nowhere is the Lordship of Christ and the way to that Lordship spelt out with greater clarity than in the kenotic hymn of the epistle to the Philippians: 'Though he was in the form of God, he did not count equality with God a thing to be grasped, but emptied himself, taking the form of a servant, being born in the likeness of men. And being found in human form he humbled himself and became obedient unto death, even death on a cross. Therefore, God has highly exalted him and bestowed on him the name which is above every name, that at the name of Jesus every knee should bow, in heaven on earth and under the earth, and every tongue confess that Jesus Christ is Lord, to the glory of God the Father' (Philippians 2:6-11). Our Christian celibacy is a special way of following Jesus by taking up the cross. It calls for a radical self-emptying in imitation of Jesus. It involves experiencing death and separation while expressing faith in resurrection and rebirth.

As celibates we must be witnesses. The original Greek word *martus*, a witness, later came to be translated as martyr. In an age of religious indifference a martyr dies not so much by shedding his blood in defence of the faith but rather in witness to Christian values. To be a witness means to live in such a way that one's life would not make sense if God did not exist. Celibacy would be a mere caricature of the Gospel if it did not make God's love visible in the community. In celebrating the Eucharist we are very conscious of the tension between what has already been achieved but we are also very conscious of what yet remains to be accomplished. Likewise as celibates we painfully experience the tension between celibacy as a grace and gift which God has given us on the one hand, and our involvement in the world on the other hand, a world which has not yet reached the fullness of salvation, and which threatens to belittle and misinterpret celibacy. Just as the Eucharist is not celebrated on a once off basis, so the choice of celibacy can never be a once only. Celibacy must be chosen over and over again whenever the alternative presents itself. I emphasize *choosing* it rather than accepting it. There is a commonly expressed attitude which runs something like this 'I did not want to be celibate, I wanted to be a priest, but since celibacy is part of the package I accept it'. Merely accepting celibacy rather than choosing it quite frequently leads to cynicism, resignation and compromise which inevitably manifests itself in living one's priesthood as a bachelor rather than a celibate.

There is a great temptation to separate celibacy and chastity. I believe that celibacy properly understood and generously lived is closely related to the three vows, poverty, chastity and obedience. Poverty is that attitude which enables the wise selection and use of things; it is a counter-sign against modern materialism. Chastity is that attitude towards others which does not manipulate them in any way but respects and nurtures them; it is a counter-sign against pleasure. Obedience is that human and humanizing attitude by which people listen carefully to and learn from the events of history and of their personal lives with a readiness to respond in a human way. It is a counter-sign against power and its abuse. Without these three attitudes human life would be diminished. We would misuse and abuse things, we would violate and manipulate others and their rights, and we would be deaf to the meaning of events as they unfold.

Our celibacy must foster the use of the gifts we have. There is one gift that is especially favoured and fostered by celibate love, namely, the gift of charity. This is the love which manifests the patience, kindness, forgiveness and trust of God himself. The celibate must acknowledge the tension which exists between the rhetoric and reality of Christian love. The reality is that the way of love is often more wearisome than wonderful. The way of love is not an emotional sentimental road, it offers no easy answers. Love does however commit the celibate to believing in an inexhaustible grace that forgives our failures and constantly empowers us to do better. In Paul's hymn to charity in 1 Corinthians 13:4-7, one could substitute the word 'the celibate' for the word 'love' and it may help to flesh out what celibacy can become. It would read something like this:

> the celibate is always patient and kind;
> the celibate is not jealous or boastful; he
> is not arrogant or rude. The celibate does
> not insist on his own way; he is not
> irritable or resentful; he does not rejoice
> at wrong, but rejoices in the right. The
> celibate bears all things, believes all
> things, hopes all things, endures all things.

If celibacy is to be a credible witness and sign, it is not the ideal which will make the impact, but the concrete living out of it. In this way confidence will replace caution and fear, and self-worth will overcome self-pity as the charism enables the priest to commit himself to a way of loving for life.

Paul's Prayer, Ephesians 3:7-21

In this prayer Paul reminds us that our ministry of the Gospel is due to God's gift and call.[15] The commission to preach the Gospel is part of the eternal plan of God and is therefore the motive of the apostle's confidence. Present afflictions therefore should not be a cause of losing heart. This prayer of intercession is an expression of faith in God. The Trinitarian character is emphasized. In praying that people 'be filled with all the fullness of God' (Ephesians 3:19) he recognizes that this will be achieved through the transforming and renewing role of the Holy Spirit which makes it possible for Christ to live in their hearts. The Apostle prays that the people *become* what they already *are* through the grace of Jesus Christ. Faith involves the submission of the total person to God's plan of love (Ephesians 1:5) as it has become known in Christ. Only when we have become 'rooted and grounded in love' therefore can we get to appreciate and appropriate God's wisdom and so live a life worthy of our calling. Only when we are endowed with a love that will make us aware of the true dimensions of the love of Christ will we be able to take part in the ultimate unravelling of God's plan and present a Gospel of hope to a despairing world.

Ephesians 3:7-21

Of this gospel I was made a minister according
to the gift of God's grace which was
given me by the working of his power. To me,
though I am the very least of all the saints,
this grace was given, to preach to the Gentiles
the unsearchable riches of Christ, and to make all
men see what is the plan of the mystery hidden
for ages in God who created all things; that
through the Church the manifold wisdom of
God might now be made known to the
principalities and powers in the heavenly
places. This was according to the eternal
purpose which he has realized in Christ
Jesus our Lord, in whom we have boldness and
confidence of access through our faith in him.
So I ask you not to lose heart over what
I am suffering for you, which is your glory.

For this reason I bow my knees before
the Father, from whom every family in heaven
and on earth is named, that according to the
riches of his glory he may grant you to be
strengthened with might through his spirit in
the inner man, and that Christ may dwell
in your hearts through faith; that you, being
rooted and grounded in love, may have
power to comprehend with all the saints what is
the breadth and length and height and depth,
and to know the love of Christ which
surpasses knowledge, that you may be filled
with all the fullness of God.

Now to him who by the power at work
within us is able to do far more abundantly
than all that we ask or think, to him be
glory in the Church and in Christ Jesus to all
generations, for ever and ever, Amen.

8

Discipleship:
From Galilee to Golgotha

A very informative insight into our vocation as priests may be obtained by reflecting on what St Mark has to say about the twelve disciples. Scholars are generally agreed that this Gospel was written about AD 68, probably in Rome, during a time of intense persecution for the followers of Christ as the grim ghost of Nero stalked the streets of that city. The evangelist is very conscious that those for whom he writes are caught in the grip of fear, yet his concern is to inspire faith. Journey, progress and pilgrimage are the outcome of faith, whereas fear is expressed in stagnation and regression. While faith enables men and women to transcend themselves, fear causes them to recoil and retreat.

Reflecting on the people Jesus chose to be his special companions – tradesmen and fishermen, tax-officials and clerks, men from the city and the country – almost every type of character is reflected in that group. You have John the believer and Thomas the one who disbelieved; there is Simon the Zealot, a fanatical nationalist. The manager of the customs house in Capernaum, Matthew the tax-collector, would have been on a commission basis, an arrangement which made crookedness almost inevitable. He would have been despised and mistrusted by fellow Jews as one who had sold out to the Roman occupation authorities. There is Peter the impulsive, a man of great generosity and personal devotion who made excessive promises, broke them, but repented. Judas, the cautious calculating character, would never have made such wild promises. Andrew comes across as the pragmatist in the group; James and John are numbered among the group; these were the ones who were blinded by ambition. How different these men are in character, attitude and action; yet they are all drawn to Jesus, surely a significant commentary on the universal nature of the Gospel.

The Call of The Twelve

Jesus did not take the line of allowing spontaneous natural leaders to stand out by themselves among the group of his followers, men who with the consent of the rest would ac-quire a directing role. The call of the twelve stands out as a fundamental initiative, a direct choice on his part: 'And he went up into the hills, and called to him those whom he desired; and they came to him' (Mark 3:13). It immediately sets up a relationship. Mark's text is very instructive: 'And he appointed twelve *to be with him* and *to be sent out to preach*' (Mark 3:14). In this twofold purpose *witness* precedes and determines *witness*. *Being with Jesus* is their primary mission. Their apostolate is founded on and derives meaning from their relationship with him. The interaction between Jesus and the twelve is very illuminating and provides today's disciple with hope. In this Gospel the disciples are constantly with Jesus. The only exception is when they are out on mission 6:14-29, and significantly during that time Jesus does not indulge in any activity, and the evangelist relates the story of the beheading of John the Baptist at that point. Once the twelve return Jesus becomes engaged again in his preaching and healing ministry.

In the narrative of the call of the twelve Jesus confers a new name on Simon, Peter. Whenever you get a name change in the Bible it expresses a new relationship with the one who changes the name, for example Abram is changed to Abraham in the Book of Genesis while Saul becomes Paul in the Acts of the Apostles. Prior to his call Peter is always named Simon in the Gospel of Mark. But after his call he is always addressed as Peter. There is one very significant exception.

Immediately before his passion Jesus impressed on his disciples the need to be alert and to watch: 'But of that day or that hour no one knows, not even the angels in heaven, nor the Son, but only the Father. Take heed, watch and pray: for you do not know when the time will come. It is like a man going on a journey, when he leaves home and puts his servants in charge, each with his work, and commands the doorkeeper to be on the watch. Watch therefore – for you do not know when the master of the house will come, in the evening, or at midnight, or at cockcrow, or in the morning   lest he come suddenly and find you asleep. And what I say to you I say to all: Watch' (Mark 13:32-37).

In Gethsemane Jesus returns from his agony to find Peter, James and John sleeping: 'and he said to Peter, *Simon*, are you asleep? Could you not watch one hour? Watch and pray that you may not enter into temptation; the spirit is willing, but the flesh is weak' (Mark 14:37-38). In other words, Peter in his failure to be alert is reverting to his pre-call state and is addressed by his old name, Simon. The evangelist emphasizes the isolation of Jesus; Judas has betrayed him, Peter has denied him, and in a final comment on their behaviour Mark says: 'and they all forsook him and fled' (14:50). In other words, the twelve deny the very first purpose for which they were called, namely 'to be with Jesus'. The disciple is one who is expected to leave everything to follow Jesus but at his arrest in Gethsemane the evangelist presents discipleship in reverse as one leaves everything to escape: 'a young man followed him, with nothing but a linen cloth about his body; and they seized him, but he left the linen cloth and ran away naked' (Mark 14:51-52).

In the face of such negative reaction one is surprised to discover that Jesus still persists with the disciples. In this Gospel every time Jesus is rejected he counteracts with a new initiative. After his rejection at Capernaum he responds with the call of the twelve. When he is rejected at Nazareth he reacts by sending the twelve out on mission. When the final let-down comes on Calvary he promises they still have a

future, he will meet them in Galilee and their failure will be
transformed and overcome.

Misunderstanding

In the first part of his ministry the disciples readily identify
with a Jesus who promises much but seems to demand little.
They misinterpret and misunderstand him. Peter their leader
is reluctant to allow Jesus to retreat for a period of quiet
prayer after a day of hectic activity, and when the leader of
the twelve finds him he reprimands him: 'everyone is searching for you' (Mark 1.37). This is the first and very subtle
indication of a disagreement between Jesus and the twelve.
Peter wants a miracle-worker who will remain at centre-
stage and who will ensure that the spotlight will continue to
shine on the group. In the eyes of the twelve Jesus could be
utilizing his time more profitably in miracle-working than in
solitary prayer. They have preconceived ideas of Jesus as a
political liberator. They will go along with him, but it is not
clear that they are prepared to *follow* him. That theme of
misunderstanding gathers momentum through the Gospel.
The disciples fail to grasp the meaning of the multiplication
of the loaves and feeding of the multitudes, of the healing of
the sick and calming of the storm. We can detect a certain
impatience and frustration building up in Jesus as he fires
rapid questions at them: 'Why do you discuss the fact that
you have no bread? Do you not yet perceive or understand?
Are your hearts hardened? Having eyes do you not see, and
having ears do you not hear? And do you not remember?
When I broke the five loaves for the five thousand, how many
baskets full of broken pieces did you take up? They said to
him, "twelve". And the seven for the four thousand, how
many baskets full of broken pieces did you take up? And
they said to him "seven". And he said to them "do you not yet
understand?" ' (Mark 8:17-21).

Journey to Jerusalem

The second part of the Gospel of Mark covers the ministry of Jesus as he leaves Galilee and moves in the direction of Jerusalem and the cross. The journey is not merely geographical; rather geography becomes a vehicle for theology. Recognizing that the disciples are only disposed towards accepting a glorious liberator Jesus proceeds to educate them in the meaning of suffering and the cross. The disciples are guilty of a lack of faith which is a form of blindness that must be healed. As the first section of the Gospel ends on a note of misunderstanding and blindness it is hardly surprising that these themes would resurface in the second part of his ministry. In a central section of his Gospel the evangelist presents Jesus instructing his disciples. Significantly that section is bracketed with two stories of the restoration of sight to blind people, the healing of the blind man at Bethsaida (8:22-26) and the healing of the blind beggar Bartimaeus (10:46-51). By framing this central section in such a way Mark has provided us with a key to interpret the material contained between these stories. The opening of eyes which occurs at the beginning and end of the section characterizes Jesus' relationship with his disciples in the intervening material. Opening the eyes of the twelve and enabling them to see is a central concern of Jesus in his instruction on the journey from Galilee to Jerusalem. What he does on behalf of the two blind men at the beginning and end of the section is what he endeavours to do for the disciples.

In the story of the blind man at Bethsaida Jesus takes him by the hand, leads him out of the village, and the miracle takes place in two stages: 'And they came to Bethsaida, and some people brought to him a blind man, and begged him to touch him. And he took the blind man by the hand, and led him out of the village; and when he had spit on his eyes and laid his hands upon him, he asked him, "do you see anything?" And he looked up and said, "I see men; but they look like trees, walking". Then again he laid his hands upon his eyes; and he looked intently and was restored, and saw everything clearly. And he sent him away to his home, saying, "do not even enter the village" ' (Mark 8:22-26). This is the only account in the New Testament which shows Jesus performing a miracle which is not complete at the first attempt. The account however is more than a description of a miracle; the story serves to illustrate the difficulty which Jesus has in removing the human blindness which is a lack of faith on the part of the disciples. In curing the blind man Jesus takes him out of the village, and away from the familiar surroundings. For someone deprived of sight this was to abandon the security of the known, of the tried and tested, and make a heroic act of faith in the one who was leading him into the unknown and the insecure. Jesus is doing something similar with the disciples as he leads them away from the success and miracle-working of Galilee and endeavours to get them to follow him in faith to Jerusalem.

In the second miracle of restoration of sight, the case of the blind beggar Bartimaeus, Mark says that having received his sight 'he *followed* him on the way'; in other words when his sight was restored he becomes a genuine disciple, illustrated by the use of a technical term for discipleship, 'to *follow*'. He *follows* Jesus on the way, that is, to Jerusalem and the Cross: 'And they came to Jericho; and as he was leaving Jericho with his disciples and a great multitude, Bartimaeus, a blind beggar, the son of Timaeus, was sitting by the roadside. And when he heard that it was Jesus of Nazareth, he began to cry out and say, "Jesus, Son of David, have mercy on me!" And many rebuked him, telling him to be silent; but he cried out all the more, "Son of David, have mercy on me!" And Jesus stopped and said, "call him". And they called the blind man, saying to him, "take heart; rise, he is calling you". And throwing off his mantle he sprang up and came to Jesus. And Jesus said to him, "what do you want me to do for you?" And the blind man said to him, "Master, let me receive my sight". And Jesus said to him, "Go your way; your faith has made you well". And immediately he received his sight and *followed him on the way*' (Mark 10:46-52).

Between these two stories of restoration of sight the misunderstanding on the part of the disciples intensifies and they begin to actually distort the meaning of Jesus' message. In more ways than one Jesus and the disciples are at *cross-purposes*. We get two manifestations of it, firstly the confession of Peter and secondly the ambition which surfaces between the disciples.

Peter's Confession

In Peter's confession all the right words are used: 'And Jesus went on with his disciples, to the villages of Caesarea Philippi; and on the way he asked his disciples, "who do men say that I am?" And they told him, "John the Baptist; and others say, Elijah; and others one of the prophets". And he asked them, "But who do you say that I am?" Peter answered him, "you are the Christ". And he charged them to tell no one about him' (Mark 8: 27-30). Jesus is the Christ, the great Messianic liberator. This confession however is something of a half truth,[16] Jesus immediately supplies the full meaning of the confession by introducing the idea of suffering: 'And he began to teach them that the Son of man must suffer many things and be rejected by the elders and the chief priests and the scribes and be killed, and after three days rise again. And he said this plainly' (Mark 8:31-32). As soon as Peter hears that suffering is part of Jesus' vocation he immediately tries to divert him from that path: 'And Peter took him and began to rebuke him' (Mark 8:32).

The Greek verb used, *epitimao*, has the connotation of muzzling; it is a quasi violent gesture and was used in the story of the cleansing of the man with the unclean spirit (Mark 1:25). In trying to prevent Jesus from following his path of suffering Mark implies that the apostle was in fact endeavouring to muzzle the Messiah. This provokes a stern reaction from Jesus: 'But turning and seeing his disciples, he rebuked Peter and said, "get behind me, Satan! For you are not on the side of God, but of men"' (Mark 8:33). This is the language of exorcism and was used by Jesus in driving out the unclean spirit in Mark 1:25 (Jesus *rebuked* him saying 'Be silent and come out of him') and also in the calming of the storm in Mark 4:39 ('and he awoke and *rebuked* the wind and said to the sea, "Peace! Be still!" and the wind ceased, and there was a great calm'). Immediately after his baptism Jesus was in the wilderness forty days, tempted by Satan (Mark 1:12-13). Here in the person of Peter Satan returns in his tempting role. Jesus uses the language of exorcism on Peter, 'he rebuked Peter and said get behind me, Satan!' (Mark 8:33) in this dramatic scene. In the Gospels Peter is the only human being who is identified as a satanic personality and he is identified as such by Jesus because he is anxious to call the shots, to dictate terms for the Messiah and decide how discipleship should be lived. The selection process is at work as Peter tries to lead Jesus into the limelight of acclaim and success which was theirs in Galilee. He must '*get behind*', that is, he must *follow* Jesus and so become a disciple. As priests we have a leadership role in the Church and we too may easily be tempted to selecting the kind of Christ who suits our own prejudices. We can parade that selection process behind very respectable banners as, like Peter, we try to chart the way for Christ rather than *follow* him.

Ambition Among the Disciples

The second manifestation of the disciples' misunderstanding may be seen in the raw ambition which surfaces among the twelve. In telling the story Mark does not give any details but you can almost hear Andrew reminding his brother Peter that it was he who pointed out the Messiah the first day, while Peter insists on his leadership role in the group. James too feels he has special claims as he belongs to the privileged triumvirate within the twelve (Peter, James and John accompany Jesus in his raising of the daughter of Jairus [Mark 5:21-43] and on the hill of transfiguration [Mark 9:2-8] and will be with him in Gethsemane [Mark 14:32-42]). Judas would probably have reminded them all that he had the purse and by implication the power. Jesus is involved in a very intense education programme. The second passion prediction is very instructive: 'They went on from there and passed through Galilee. And he would not have any one know it; for he was teaching his disciples saying to them, "The Son of man will be delivered into the hands of men, and they will kill him; and when he is killed, after three days he will rise"' (Mark 9:30-31). All priests have experienced the frustration of conscientiously preparing a homily, a class or a talk only to discover that the central point has escaped the congregation and they take to the tangential. Having spelt out specifi cally for the second time his future suffering Mark conveys the reaction of the disciples in a single sentence: 'But they did not understand the saying, and they were afraid to ask him' (Mark 9:32).

These two motifs, lack of perception and fearful inhibition to ask for an explanation, reinforce each other and deepen the disciples' dilemma. Immediately after the second passion prediction we find the disciples discussing with one another who was the greatest (Mark 9:34), indicating that they are on a totally different wave-length. Personal power and prestige is their primary preoccupation. This results in a domineering and exclusive mentality on their part. They are anxious to ensure that exorcism will be an exclusive preserve of their own and so they endeavour to prevent an exorcist from functioning because he is not one of their number (Mark 9:38-41). They try to dominate Jesus by deciding who will have access to him. Although Jesus had emphasized the importance of receiving the kingdom as a little child (Mark 9:36-37), the disciples try, but fail, to prevent people from bringing little children to him for a blessing (Mark 10:13-16). Their personal ambition in the face of Jesus' foretelling of his suffering and death reveals a utilitarian attachment to a glorious and powerful Messiah. Their preoccupation is with power and prestige so they cannot hear what Jesus is saying.

The third passion prediction is the most explicit: 'Behold, we are going up to Jerusalem; and the Son of man will be delivered to the chief priests and the scribes, and they will condemn him to death, and deliver him to the gentiles; and they will mock him, and spit upon him, and scourge him, and kill him; and after three days he will rise' (Mark 10:33-34). It is as if Jesus summons up all his reserves in this final supreme effort to initiate the disciples. What will the response be on this occasion? James and John in keeping with their previous approach make a request for positions of power. When they approach Jesus he asks: 'What do you want me to do for you' (Mark 10:32).

That very same question in identical words was put by Jesus to the blind Bartimaeus in Jericho (Mark 10:51), but whereas the latter answers: 'Master, let me receive my sight' (Mark 10:51), James and John respond: 'Grant us to sit, one at your right-hand and one at your left, in your glory' (Mark 10:37). The blind man requests sight, the faith which will enable him to follow Jesus on the way to Jerusalem while James and John plot and plan a glorious future for themselves.

The disciples then are portrayed as incorrigible and obtuse. Each passion-prediction evokes a response which is selfish and self-centred. While Jesus speaks of his suffering and death, the disciples dream of personal power and prestige. Anxious self-concern and success prevents them from hearing what Jesus is saying. They react as men who wish to acquire the world and lord it over others. They are a combination of faith and fear. The opposite of faith in the Bible is fear rather than doubt. Like Peter in the Gospel of Matthew they are prepared to go some distance towards meeting Jesus but are overcome by fear: 'But when the disciples saw him walking on the sea, they were terrified, saying, "It is a ghost!" And they cried out for fear. But immediately he spoke to them, saying, "Take heart, it is I; have no fear". And Peter answered him, "Lord, if it is you, *bid me come* to you on the water". He said, "*come*". So Peter got out of the boat and walked on the water and came to Jesus; but when he saw the wind, he *was afraid*, and beginning to sink he cried out, "Lord, save me" ' (Matthew 14:28-30).

During the passion fear on the part of the disciples reaches a crescendo. After the arrest Peter follows Jesus at a distance into the courtyard of the high priest. They separate and the camera focuses firstly on the trial of Jesus upstairs. The high priest questions him: 'Are you the Christ, the Son of the Blessed?' (Mark 14:61) to which Jesus replies 'I am' (14:62). At the same time in the courtyard below there is a close-up shot of Peter warming himself at the fire. When challenged by one of the servants of the high priest with being a disciple of Jesus, 'you also were *with* the Nazarene' (Mark 14:67). Peter is at first evasive: 'I neither know nor understand what you mean' (14:68). When the challenge persists he at first denies being one of Jesus' followers but when the pressure is really applied he begins to curse and swear, and vehemently denies and disowns Jesus: 'I do not know this man of whom you speak' (Mark 14:71). So at the very moment when Jesus identifies with men, Peter denies his discipleship. Fear expresses itself in betrayal for Judas, in denial for the leader of the twelve, and in flight for all of the disciples.

Faith and Fear

Faith courageously sets out on the journey towards the promised land, fear causes us to lay hold of any support we may find and use it as a crutch. While faith provides the courage to let go, fear forces us to cling. The disciples' call is to follow Jesus. When the inner group had abandoned him Mark presents the women as fulfilling the requirements for discipleship, they ministered to him and followed him from Galilee to Golgotha. The evangelist is careful to note that the women were witnesses not only of Jesus' death but also of his burial place (15:47) and later of the empty tomb (16:5). These were the women: 'who when he was in *Galilee, followed* him, and *ministered* to him; and also many other women who came up *with him* to *Jerusalem*' (Mark 15:40-41).

That is the journey which we too have to make, from Galilee to Jerusalem. Priests, like the disciples in St Mark's Gospel are a combination of faith and fear. We are called to follow Jesus and sent to serve others. Today in the Church the stable is shot through with the unstable, the predictable with the unpredictable. We have to be courageous, face up to and live with our deepest doubts, our nagging anxieties, and inadequacies. We have to respond positively and eagerly to the unusual and unexpected. We have to be prepared to try new methods and experiment with pastoral initiatives. In doing so we have to take many decisions on our own and cope with the resulting loneliness and anguish. We are conscious of the possibility of error, failure, and ignominy because we take risks, but we cannot afford not to take them.

The programme of discipleship is our programme as we return to the task of not giving up on the difficult and demanding. We may ask ourselves a few questions as priests. Have I got things all out of proportion? Have I accepted a call which demands that I give myself to others and am less preoccupied with my success and failure? In my priesthood have I separated the table of the Eucharistic sacrifice and the towel of service which Jesus united in the Last Supper scene in John Chapter 13? Because of his responsibility the priest runs the risk – certainly unconsciously – of making an idol of his own virtue, real or presumed, of turning the gift of the Gospel into his own human achievement of which he may boast like the Pharisee in Luke 18:9-14. There is the great temptation facing all of us, not to accept the past, to try to control the present and to look to the future with fear and apprehension. Everything which cannot be packaged or programmed causes anxiety and worry. We have to abandon the pretence of knowing everything, of having all the answers, while being free from the fear of knowing nothing. What about the times when I took first place and Christ retreated to second, when I lived under the illusion that I was opening minds and hearts and healing hurts but ignored the words of Jesus: 'apart from me you can do nothing?' (John 15:5).

Have I committed myself forever to God's call or am I subconsciously influenced by the current climate of opinion which proposes a theology of temporary vocation. The one who does not commit himself forever only lends himself and remains an adolescent. An adult is one who is able to give himself definitively without breaking the word he had given and, in spite of his fear and failure, he can continue to love because for him apostolic succession is more important than apostolic success. Admitting and accepting our limitations is not a passive act, something done with resentful resignation. It is a positive and creative approach to our situation. The Church will survive heresy and hatred, sin and persecution. What is dangerous is the lukewarm priest. It is not sufficient to re-present the crucified Christ liturgically. The liturgy expresses ritually what takes place in the rest of my life. The question is, does it?

The Priestly Prayer of Christ John 17

The concluding words of John 16:33: 'In the world you have tribulation; but courage, I have overcome the world' form a fitting transition to the prayer of Jesus which follows. This prayer is closely related to the farewell discourses and farewell blessings of the patriarchs in the Old Testament. Moses, turning his eyes to heaven, invokes the blessing of the Lord at the end of a lengthy farewell discourse to the elders in Deuteronomy 32-33. It is significant that all the prayers of Jesus which have been transmitted to us in the Gospels begin with the word 'Father', for example Matthew 11:25, Mark 14:36, Luke 23:34, 46. Addressing God as Father here in John 17 creates the climate for the prayer which sums up the ministry and message of Jesus. While the Synoptic Gospels frequently present Jesus in prayer to his Father it is only on very rare occasions that the reader is given an insight into the actual content of his prayer. In Gethsemane the Synoptics present the prayer of Jesus as concentrating on obedience through suffering, but the fourth Gospel while underpinning the obedience of Jesus to the Father's will does not allude to sorrow or sadness in his prayer.

The chapter may be divided into four sections.

● In the first part (v.1-5) Jesus, addressing the Father, prays that his approaching death will be the means by which he glorifies the Father and will be glorified by the Father. Glory is one of the key concepts of the Bible and of Christian prayer. It expresses that which is constitutive of God's being and at the same time it denotes the honour which is due to God.

● In the second section (v.6-19) Jesus prays for the disciples gathered around him. The word *mathêtês* (disciple) occurs with greater frequency in the fourth Gospel than in any other Gospel, an indication that for this evangelist the idea of discipleship is very important. The close bond between the community of believers and Jesus is central to John's concept of the Church and not surprisingly it becomes a concern of the prayer of Jesus. This community has been chosen and called by God and to this group will be entrusted the fulfilment of Jesus' mission. At an early stage in the Gospel the purpose of Jesus' mission had been stated: 'For God so loved the world that he gave his only Son, that whoever believes in him should not perish but have eternal life. For God sent the Son into the world, not to condemn the world, but that the world might be saved through him' (John 3:16-17). That purpose will be realized through the community of disciples, but because of the hostility of the world they will be open to attack as the power of evil divides, undermines, and sows seeds of suspicion and strife. The way of the disciples will be the way of Jesus which is the way of the cross. There will be a strong temptation for disciples to seek for safety and security in separation from the world. Jesus does not ask his Father to take the disciples out of the world but requests that He should keep them from the evil one. Since there can be no gnostic withdrawal from the world, which is under the influence of the power of evil, Jesus prays that his disciples will be kept safe from the power of the evil one. This petition is similar to that of the Lord's prayer in Matthew 6:13: 'But deliver us from evil'. While Jesus has taken up a position against the evil one in his death on the cross the disciples must do likewise. Just as the Father had consecrated Jesus for his mission (John 10:36) so now Jesus prays that the Father will consecrate the disciples for theirs. They will be equipped by the truth which is God's word. The disciples are sanctified for their mission in the world by Jesus' sacrificial death on the cross.

● In the third part (v.20-24) the prayer is extended to later generations of disciples who are dependent on the word of the apostles. Their unity will be a way of evangelizing the world since it will make people conscious of the claim of Jesus as one sent by the Father. The unity of the disciples is based on and derives from the unity of the Father and Son and is not the result of human effort. The unity of the Father and Son is a unity of love, likewise the unity of believers is to be one of love which will prove to the world that God has loved them. The final destiny of all disciples is to live with Christ in the eternal world and behold his glory.

● The final section (v.25-26) summarizes the result of Jesus' ministry. In contrast to the ignorance of the world the disciples know that Jesus was sent by the Father. The disciples live in hope and longing but in a serene confidence because they have already experienced the revelation of the Father's love in Jesus. Love, proceeding from the Father as its primordial source, is the bond which unites the Father and the Son with the disciples. Jesus is not only the mediator of God's love for the disciples but also the constant presence of God among them. In many respects the whole of the Gospel is concentrated in this prayer of Jesus.

John 17

When Jesus had spoken these words, he lifted up his eyes to heaven and said, 'Father, the hour has come; glorify thy Son that the Son may glorify thee, since thou hast given him power over all flesh, to give eternal life to all whom thou hast given him. And this is eternal life, that they know thee the only true God, and Jesus Christ whom thou hast sent. I glorified thee on earth, having accomplished the work which thou gavest me to do; and now,

Father, glorify thou me in thy own presence with the glory
which I had with thee before the world was made.

'I have manifested thy name to the men whom thou gavest
me out of the world; thine they were, and thou gavest them
to me, and they have kept thy word. Now they know that
everything that thou hast given me is from thee; for I have
given them the words which thou gavest me, and they have
received them and know in truth that I came from thee; and
they have believed that thou didst send me. I am praying
for them; I am not praying for the world but for those
whom thou hast given me, for they are thine; all mine
are thine, and thine are mine, and I am glorified in them.
And now I am no more in the world, but they are in the
world, and I am coming to thee. Holy Father, keep them in
thy name, which thou hast given me, that they may be one,
even as we are one. While I was with them, I kept them
in thy name, which thou hast given me; I have guarded them,
and none of them is lost but the son of perdition, that the
scripture might be fulfilled. But now I am coming to thee;
and these things I speak in the world, that they may have
my joy fulfilled in themselves. I have given them thy
word; and the world has hated them because they are not
of the world. I do not pray that thou shouldst take them
out of the world, but that thou shouldst keep them from
the evil one. They are not of the world, even as I am not
of the world. Sanctify them in the truth; thy word is truth.
As thou didst send me into the world, so I have sent them
into the world. And for their sake I consecrate myself,
that they also may be consecrated in truth.

'I do not pray for these only, but also for those who
believe in me through their word, that they may all be one;
even as thou, Father, art in me, and I in thee, that they also
may be in us, so that the world may believe that thou hast
sent me. The glory which thou hast given me I have given
to them, that they may be one even as we are one, I in them
and thou in me, that they may become perfectly one, so that
the world may know that thou hast sent me and hast loved
them even as thou hast loved me. Father, I desire that they
also, whom thou hast given me, may be with me where I am,
to behold my glory which thou hast given me in thy love for

DISCIPLESHIP: FROM GALILEE TO GOLGOTHA   109

me before the foundation of the world. O righteous Father, the world has not known thee, but I have known thee; and these know that thou hast sent me. I made known to them thy name, and I will make it known that the love with which thou hast loved me may be in them, and I in them.'

9

Eucharist: Remembering and Reconciliation

In the priestly account of creation God created the heavenly luminaries: 'And God said, Let there be lights in the firmament of the heavens to separate the day from the night; and let them be for signs and for seasons and for days and for years, and let them be lights in the firmament of the heavens to give light upon the earth. And it was so' (Genesis 1:14-15). They are created to mark time for us. Through the solar and lunar cycles God makes us aware of time, of birthdays and anniversaries. The ability to measure time is a gift of God in creation. Measuring time is strictly related to memory which enables us to make present events which are remote in space or time. The memory of special events is brought to life in festive celebrations. When the Israelites settled in the Promised Land they remembered and reflected on their previous experience as semi-nomads and particularly on the liberation which God had granted them in the exodus. The community participated in the festive celebrations which Passover, Unleavened Bread and Tabernacles commemorated. Passover turns the minds and hearts to the final, permanent deliverance from evil. It is a 'feast of challenge' in which God intervenes and challenges oppressive relationships and idolatry.[17] In this the Israelites considered themselves to be in solidarity with their ancestors. Memory is of the utmost importance for a pilgrim people, without it or through neglect of it people are deprived of their past, forfeit the future, and are confined to the present. The Book of Deuteronomy, which envisages the people on the threshold of the land of Canaan being addressed in most solemn terms by Moses, highlights the importance of remembering. This task is part of an historical process of rendering ancient tradition accessible to future generations. It is calculated to ensure that the people look on the past as a history of divine favours and on the future as containing both promises and threats.

Refusal to Remember

The sociological change from a semi-nomadic to a settled community would make new and unforeseen demands on the faith of the people. For that reason the speech of Moses is filled with promise and demand. While the land is a gift of God it is also a situation full of temptation because the urban and rural culture of its inhabitants is regarded as being under the protection of the numerous gods of the Canaanites. In remembering the greatness and mercy of God they will find security for the present and hope for the future. The real danger is that they will forget the Lord and endeavour to invent their own independent identity and so lose security in the present and will be reduced to looking on the future with despair. Memory is the chief resource for Israel in resisting these temptations. The gift of economic prosperity becomes a great temptation if the Giver is forgotten. The producer-consumer cycle is seen as self-explanatory as God disappears from the horizon. As a result they cease to be a historical people, open either to the Lord of history or to his blessings yet to be given. They will model themselves on the surrounding pagan nations adopting their ways. At the moment of entry into the land Joshua makes a characteristic appeal: 'Be strong and very courageous, being careful to do according to all the law which Moses my servant commanded you; turn not from it to the right hand or to the left, that you may have good success wherever you go. This book of the law shall not depart out of your mouth, but you shall meditate on it day and night, that you may be careful to do according to all that is written in it; for then you shall make your way prosperous, and then you shall have good success' (Joshua 1:7-8).

What is required therefore is courage to keep the Torah. Torah is precisely to preserve memory for those who are tempted to forget. It is not to cramp behaviour, not to coerce or control but to keep Israel in its historical relationship with the Lord. It is calculated to ensure that mystery is not manipulated or reduced to manageable size: 'Take heed lest you forget the Lord who brought you out of the land of Egypt' (Deuteronomy 6:12): 'Take heed lest you forget the Lord your God, by not keeping his commandments and his ordinances and his statutes' (Deuteronomy 8:11). We are reaping the whirlwind in our society today. We played down the importance of the Torah and as a result people forgot the Lord and the way was open for widespread exploitation, manipulation and greed. One example of this may be seen in the violation of the Sabbath. In Israel the Sabbath affirmed that people cannot be possessed or managed; it draws lines of dignity, respect, and freedom around them in a protective way. Violation of the Sabbath whether then or now reduces people to the role of producer-consumer.

Failure to remember is a form of ingratitude; memory is thanksgiving, Eucharist.[18] The temptation which faced Israel confronts Christians in a similar way, the temptation to forget the Lord and what he has achieved for us in Jesus Christ. For Christians memory, thanksgiving, must involve Christ. It is significant that the Eucharist is the only thing which Jesus asks us to do in memory of him: 'And he took bread, and when he had given thanks he broke it and gave it to them, saying, "this is my body which is given for you. *Do this in remembrance of me*" ' (Luke 22:19). Our celebration of Eucharist ensures we have a living memory, not just some vague, nebulous recollection. Central to that memory is the death and resurrection of Jesus Christ: 'Father, we celebrate the *memory* of Christ, your Son. We, your people and your ministers, recall his passion, his resurrection from the dead, and his ascension into glory; and from the many gifts you have given us we offer you, God of glory and majesty...' (The Roman Canon).

As we have seen in chapter three, the people of the Old Testament lived between a memory and an anticipation, between an exodus in the past and a definitive exodus in the future. Their celebration of passover always gave expression to this twofold emphasis on past and future. We are more familiar with memory of the past but there is also a memory, a reminder, of the future. Hope gives expression to this memory of the future; it is to make the future present. For the Christian the promise of the past orientates us towards the future: 'This Jesus, who was taken up from you into heaven, will come in the same way as you saw him go into heaven' (Acts 1:11). After the consecration we are invited to proclaim the *mystery of faith*. The acclamation then does justice to past, present and future: 'Christ *has died*, Christ *is risen*, Christ *will come* again.' The celebration of the Eucharist occurs between the memory of Christ's first coming and the memory which is a hope of the final coming, between the past and the *parousia*.

Memory and the Future

In the Emmaus story (Luke 24:13-35) we get a close-up of two disciples whose memory is merely a recollection of the past, but has no present vitality and no hope for the future.[19] Because of their concentration on the past they can salvage nothing from it and their perspective is totally inadequate. The experience of the disciples on the Emmaus road is one shared by all followers of Jesus Christ. They are leaving Jerusalem prior to the descent of the Holy Spirit who would lead them into all truth (John 16:13). Because of this they have a very inadequate understanding of Jesus Christ and particularly of the disconcerting facts of the previous week. They despair because having invested so much in their following of Jesus they feel it has all gone aground on Golgotha. They are disillusioned because their hopes for political liberation have been dashed: 'We *had* hoped that he was the one to redeem Israel' (Luke 24:21). This was all now past tense, it is the language of failure and hurt rather than faith and happiness. They are confused by the report of some women claiming that Jesus was alive, which was supported by some disciples who found the tomb empty.

There is a conversion experience on the Emmaus road when these two disciples invite Jesus into their lives and provide him with an opportunity to clarify their thoughts and disentangle their confused minds. The comment of the disciples is a bit like Peter's confession which we examined in the previous chapter. They have the terminology, indeed the words which will be used by the early Christian preachers in proclaiming the Gospel: 'Jesus of Nazareth, who was a prophet mighty in deed and word before God and all the people, and how our chief priests and rulers delivered him up to be condemned to death and crucified him. But we had hoped that he was the one to redeem Israel. Yes, and besides all this, it is now the third day since all this happened. Moreover, some women of our company amazed us. They were at the tomb early in the morning and did not find his body; and they came back saying that they had seen a vision of angels, who said that he was alive. Some of those who were with us went to the tomb, and found it just as the women had said; but him they did not see' (Luke 24:19-24).

They have all the essentials of the Christian Gospel, Jesus was handed over by the chief priests, condemned to death, the finding of the empty tomb, and the news that Jesus is alive. What the disciples fail to see is that all this is in keeping with and determined by the plan of God. This dimension will be recognized by Peter in his speech in the Acts of the Apostles, Chapter 2: 'this Jesus, delivered up according to the definite plan and foreknowledge of God, you crucified and killed by the hands of lawless men. But God raised him up, having loosened the pangs of death' (Acts 2:23-24). Jesus recognizes that the disciples need to be jolted if they are to be liberated from the grip of despair and disappointment: 'O foolish men, and slow of heart to believe all that the prophets have spoken' (Luke 24:25). Once they are released from their self-preoccupations Jesus sets about explaining the scriptures to them: 'Was it not necessary that the Christ should suffer these things and enter into his glory?' (Luke 24:26).

The all too human events take on a new dimension once the perspective of the plan of God is supplied. We can readily identify with these disciples when we are faced with an eclipse of God in our lives and wonder why he does not show his hand in new and strange situations when well-laid hopes come to nothing and we feel frustrated and have to do a complete re-think on the meaning of God's will. In such situations it is understandable to experience self-pity, to yield to scepticism and defeatism.

With the aid of scripture Jesus explains God's plan. This is basically a liturgy of the word which precedes and prepares for the Eucharistic meal: 'And beginning with Moses and all the prophets, he interpreted to them in all the scriptures the things concerning himself' (Luke 24:27). Like these disciples we too need to have our vision adjusted and our reading of events corrected by Christ, otherwise we too will jump to conclusions as confusion, defeatism, and frustration take over. For Israel the desert had been a time of waiting and purification. What characterizes that time is hope and active perseverance. By contrast inactive waiting becomes a form of imprisonment and in the case of the disciples on the Emmaus road it expresses itself in impatience and frustration. An essential aspect of Christianity is a certain dynamism, an eschatological tension. The danger is that we cease to expect more, we become content to conserve and repeat.

Breaking of Bread and Brokenness

In the breaking of the bread Jesus makes himself known to them. The term breaking of bread is one of the earliest ways of describing the Eucharist. In 1 Corinthians we find the earliest literary evidence for the Eucharist where Paul says: 'I received from the Lord what I also delivered to you that the Lord Jesus on the night when he was betrayed took bread, and when he had given thanks, he broke it, and said, "this is my body which is broken for you. Do this in remembrance of me" ' (1 Corinthians 11:23-24). It is significant that Jesus comes to the Eucharist a betrayed and broken man. Yet in that very situation he gives thanks to the Father: 'The Lord Jesus on the night when he was *betrayed*, took bread, and when he had *given thanks* ' (1 Corinthians 11:23-24).

Priests frequently come to the Eucharist broken men and often times betrayed. Failure to achieve our goals, disappointment when others fail to reach the standards we had set for them, disillusionment with circumstances – all of these make us restless and unhappy, creating the illusion that we are at the centre of our world and everything revolves around us. In moments like these we look for the consolations of God rather than the God of consolations. It is extremely difficult and demanding in those situations to lift up our hearts and to invite others to lift up theirs as we move into the preface of the Mass. The Eucharist however is precisely for such wounded people and broken hearts; the self-righteous and self-sufficient feel they have no need of Eucharist. After all is not Eucharist *thanksgiving* and *praise*, the same Hebrew word covered both. One of the results of thanksgiving/praise is to take the focus and the pressure off ourselves, to become orientated towards God, placing him at the centre. In this way we get the perspective right, and the Eucharist has a liberating quality freeing us from a morbid preoccupation with ourselves. This is all the more important as we live in a consumerist society where the pressure is on us to be achievers. The action in the Emmaus meal is unmistakably Eucharistic: 'When he was at table with them, he *took* the bread and *blessed* and *broke* it, and *gave* it to them' (Luke 24:30) – actions reminiscent of the Last Supper: 'And he *took* bread, and when he had *given thanks* he *broke* it and *gave* it to them' (Luke 22:19). As a result of the Eucharist: 'Their eyes were opened and they recognized him' (Luke 24:31).

The opening of eyes is a part of a process of rebirth and reconciliation; eyes which had been blinded by the traffic of years now open again with the eagerness and innocence of childhood. The disciples returned to Jerusalem after their meeting with the risen Lord in the breaking of bread. When we come to turning points in our lives and refuse to turn we get warped instead. We have witnessed people and institutions getting warped in situations where they might repent or readjust.

Bread must have had a special significance for Jesus. Born in Bethlehem which in Hebrew means *house of bread* Jesus must have reflected on how one day bread would become the vehicle of his presence to mankind. During his Galilean ministry we find him feeding the multitudes, five thousand, seven thousand, with bread in ways which have an undeniable Eucharistic tone: 'And *taking* the five loaves and the two fish he looked up to heaven, and *blessed* and *broke* them, and *gave* them to the disciples to set before the crowd' (Luke 9:16-17).

The land does not produce bread directly. The first mention of bread in scripture occurs with reference to the sweat of one's brow (Genesis 3:19). Bread is a creation of man involving his human contribution. Where you find bread you find people. We witness the anxiety around us today when the breadwinner has no work. Jesus was concerned that people would have bread to eat. With his down-to-earth care for people's everyday life, he included in the Lord's prayer the petition: 'Give us each day our daily bread' (Luke 11:3).

In the humble the sublime is revealed: 'Blessed are you, Lord God of all creation. Through your goodness we have this bread to offer, which earth has given and human hands have made. It will become for us the bread of life' (Offertory of the Mass). The Father accepts our humble gifts, to change them into glorified ones. Wheat is ground down, as Christ was ground down, made into bread and delivered to mankind in a life-sustaining way, as Christ was fully delivered for them, and returns to deliver himself having been made bread.

We have seen how God disciplined his people time and again, for example Moses in the sojourn in Egypt, Elijah at the time of the threat of the nature religions, and the chosen people in the Babylonian exile. He does this in order to bring them to deeper faith in himself and to a fuller realization of their own identity. He had to 'break' them. So too with ourselves, to make us mediators of his salvation God 'breaks' us so that we become more effective ministers in his service. Paradoxically I am least myself when I take myself too seriously, when the days and nights revolve around me, around my delights and worries, my dreams and my fears. As priests it is our responsibility to point to Christ and yet our ideas of Christ are in constant need of correction and revision. It is not always easy to recognize Christ. He comes in unexpected ways, for which we are not prepared. Like the Emmaus travellers we too are taken by surprise and, quite frequently, it is this surprise which reminds us that we are instruments, that we must decrease so that Christ would increase. Christ does with me precisely what he did with the bread; he *takes* me, *blesses, breaks* me and *gives* me. The broken bread has a healing and liberating force. But in order that the bread be given it must first be broken. Like bread, we as priests are given to others in colleges, parishes and hospitals, and are intended to be a liberating force and a healing influence for the oppressed and enslaved. But before and in our being given we experience brokenness. In this we recognize not a God who keeps us out of trouble but rather a God who is our support in trouble. Like the disciples at Emmaus our eyes are also opened in the breaking, whether it is the bread or ourselves that is broken, and we recognize Jesus Christ and see reality with the eyes of Christ and so are enabled to open the eyes of others as we respond to their human cry. In our relationship with God we experience moments of ecstasy and fulfilment but also moments of rejection and despair, cruel separation and agonizing reconciliation. Opening of eyes is part of the process of reconciliation and rebirth.

In the celebration of the Emmaus meal Jesus liberated two people from slavery as they wallowed in confusion and bitterness, enslaved by yesterday, disappointed by the present and despairing of the future. Priests have a particular responsibility for liberating others from a similar slavery to self, enabling them to cast themselves in faith and trust on God. We begin every Eucharist with a penitential rite as we invite people to recognize the ways in which they are enslaved and repent of what deprives them of peace. With the aid of Scripture we endeavour to interpret events for them as we unfold God's plan into which they too have been inserted. There they recognize the scandal of the cross, both Christ's and their own. In the breaking of bread we attempt to open their eyes, giving them a new vision which will remove and resist all oppressive relationships, so that they are liberated from fear and will in all circumstances be people with a new future and a hope that gives life as they oppose what is untrue and has no future. We conclude the Eucharist by bidding them go in the peace of Christ as free men and free women.

Psalm 23

The Lord is My Shepherd

This psalm is characterized by a serenity which emanates from trust in God. In a liturgical service the psalmist experiences the peace which comes from communion with the Lord. It is one of the most popular and has rightly been described as the 'pearl of the psalms'. Its simplicity could easily conceal its richness. Two key word-pictures dominate, firstly the Lord as a tender caring shepherd and secondly the Lord as a gracious host. The decisive point is found at the very centre of the psalm:[20] 'you are there' (in Hebrew 'you are with me') and this relates both to what has preceded, the image of the shepherd, and what follows, the image of the host.

In the Old Testament the metaphor of the Lord as shepherd is a frequent one. In the traditions of the exodus God is presented as shepherding his flock in the desert. In the psalm the imagery is developed concisely in a few very evocative scenes:

Fresh and green are the pastures
where he gives me repose.
Near restful waters he leads me,
to revive my drooping spirit. . .

and words which suggest the pastoral life, namely, the 'right path', 'valley of darkness', 'crook and staff'. Journeying through the valley with the approach of nightfall the sheep with their poor sense of direction derive security from the recognized sound of the shepherd's staff on the rock, while the crook by which he rescues the stray provides a reassuring presence. While these things are predicated of the shepherd and his sheep there is a very personal note introduced as the psalmist abandons the third person for the second: 'you are there.' In this second person we recognize the authentic shepherd, the Lord. What has been said of the shepherd and the flock are now seen as applicable to the Lord and his people as he guides us along the way which he has trodden and provides us with security and serenity in the midst of threat.

The metaphor in the second part of the poem changes from that of shepherd and sheep to a word-picture of host and guest. In a semi-nomadic culture the hospitality of the tent provided safety for those pursued by enemies. While one enjoys the hospitality of his host the enemies dare not attack. The psalmist may have been influenced by his experience in the temple, where the sacrificial meal followed the sacrifice of thanksgiving. God, as the psalmist's host, offers the sacrificial meal to his faithful who had already offered their lives in obedience to him. In that same temple service one's enemies would also be present. The temple is the tent of hospitality where the attributes of the covenant God, 'goodness and kindness', are experienced. The serenity which he experiences there will accompany him right through his life.

Although the images of shepherd and host are separate they may be united through the traditions of the exodus. In their departure from Egypt God led his people through the wilderness, providing them with water, food and rest. When they reach the promised land the Lord welcomes them as a host. As we read the psalm against the New Testament background where Jesus is presented as the true shepherd John 10:1-18 we find the christological and ecclesial dimensions are united. In Christ the 'goodness and kindness' of God become manifest and are now available in the Church for the pilgrim people. In our journey we experience in the sacraments, among other institutions, comfort and consolation, the life-giving water of Baptism, and the sustaining influence of the Eucharistic chalice and bread as well as the anointing with oil. In the early Church this psalm was used at the Easter vigil when the newly baptised, coming from the Baptismal font, were anointed with oil and led to the Eucharistic table for the first time.

Psalm 23

The Lord is my shepherd;
there is nothing I shall want.
Fresh and green are the pastures
where he gives me repose.
Near restful waters he leads me,
to revive my drooping spirit.

He guides me along the right path;
he is true to his name.
If I should walk in the valley of darkness
no evil would I fear.
You are there with your crook and your staff;
with these you give me comfort.

You have prepared a banquet for me
in the sight of my foes.
My head you have anointed with oil;
my cup is overflowing.

Surely goodness and kindness shall follow me
all the days of my life.
In the Lord's own house shall I dwell
for ever and ever.

Notes

1. Luis Alonso Schökel has drawn attention to covenant motifs of Genesis 2-3 in *Pentateuco*, Los Libros Sagrados, Volume I, Ediciones Cristianidad, Madrid 1970, 26-27; also in Motivos Sapienciales Y De Alianza en Gen. 2-3, *Biblica* 43(1962), pp. 295-315.
2. David J. A. Clines, *The Theme of the Pentateuch*, Journal for the Study of the Old Testament Supplement Series 10, Sheffield 1984, 65 – Recognizing the spread of sin Clines sees the theme 'creation – uncreation – recreation' as central to Genesis 1-11, pp. 74-76.
3. Carlo M. Martini has an extensive treatment of the various stages of Moses' life in *Vita di Mosè*, Edizioni Borla, Rome 1981, 15-28.
4. Luis Alonso Schökel, *Salvacion Y Liberacion, Cuadernos Biblicos 5, Valencia 1980*, p. 54.
5. Walter Brueggemann, *The Land*, Fortress Press, Philadelphia, 1977, pp. 63-65.
6. John Gray, *I and II Kings*, Old Testament library, SCM Press, London 1977, p. 376.
7. Luis Alonso Schökel, *Reyes*, Ediciones Christianidad, Madrid 1973, p. 124.
8. Walter Brueggemann, *Praying The Psalms*, St. Mary's Press, Minnesota 1986, p. 20, uses the orientation – disorientation – reorientation framework to interpret the Psalms of Lament. I find these concepts particularly applicable to the exile experience.
9. Walter Burghardt, *Tell The Next Generation*, Paulist Press, New York 1980, p. 105.
10. Scholars are generally agreed that Isaiah 40-55 was not written by the prophet Isaiah of the eight century BC. They consider Deutero-Isaiah to be an anonymous prophet who experienced the Babylonian exile and witnessed the turbulent condition which prevailed between the destruction of Jerusalem in 587 and the downfall of the Persian Empire in 539.
11. Luis Alonso Schökel/J.L. Sicre Diag, *Profetas*, Volume I, Ediciones

Cristianidad, Madrid 1980, pp. 268, 295.

12. Walter Burghardt, *Sir we would like to see Jesus,* Paulist Press, New York 1982, pp. 203-204.

13 Carlo M. Martini, *La Donna nel Suo Populo,* Editrice Ancora, Milano 1987, pp. 36-37.

14. Joyce Ridick, *Treasures in Earthenware Vessels: The Vows,* St Paul Publications, Slough 1984, pp. 55-56 lists some useful criteria for evaluating friendships.

15. The letter to the Ephesians was written, whether by Paul himself or by one of his closest disciples, at a time when the Apostle's work for the unity of Jews and Gentiles in the Church was becoming an accomplished fact. The question raised by the authorship is ultimately of little importance beside the richness of the ideas which find expression in the letter.

16. Augustine Stock, *Call to Discipleship,* Veritas Publications, Dublin 1982, pp. 130-132.

17. Xavier Leon-Dufour, *Sharing The Eucharist Bread,* Paulist Press, New York 1987, p. 192.

18. Luis Alonso Schökel, *Celebrating the Eucharist,* St Paul Publications, Slough 1988, p. 98.

19. Carlo M. Martini provides an excellent treatment of the Emmaus story in *Ministers of the Gospel,* St Paul Publications, Slough 1983, pp. 20-39.

20. Gianfranco Ravasi, *Il Libro dei Salmi,* vol 1, Editione Dehoniane, Bologna 1986, pp. 430-431.

Bibliography

Alonso Schökel, Luis, *Treinta Salmos: Poesia Y Oracion*, Institucion San Jeronimo, Valencia 1981.

Los Libros Sagrados, Ediciones Cristianidad, Madrid, 1966-1975.

Profetas, 2 Volumes, Madrid 1980.

Salvacion Y Liberacion, Cuadernos Biblicos 5 Valencia 1980.

Celebrating The Eucharist, St Paul Publications, Slough 1988.

Brueggemann, Walter, *The Land*, Fortress Press, Philadelphia 1977.

Praying The Psalms, St Mary's Press, Minnesota 1986.

Burghardt, Walter J. *Sir We Would Like To See Jesus*, Paulist Press, New York 1982. *Tell The Next Generation*, Paulist Press, New York 1980.

Clines, David J.A. *The Theme of the Pentateuch*, Journal for the Study of The Old Testament Series, 10, Sheffield 1984.

Leon-Dufour, Xavier, *Sharing The Eucharistic Bread*, Paulist Press, New York 1987.

Martini, Carlo M. *La Donna nel Suo Populo*, Editrice Ancora, Milano 1987.

Ministers of The Gospel, St Paul Publications, Slough 1983. *Vita di Mose*, Edizioni Borla, Rome 1981.

Ravasi, Gianfranco, *Il Libro dei Salmi*, 3 vols, Editione Dehoniane, Bologna, 1986.

Ridick, Joyce, *Treasures in Earthen Vessels : The Vows*, St Paul Publications, Slough 1984.

Stock, Augustine, *Call To Discipleship*, Veritas Publications, Dublin 1982.